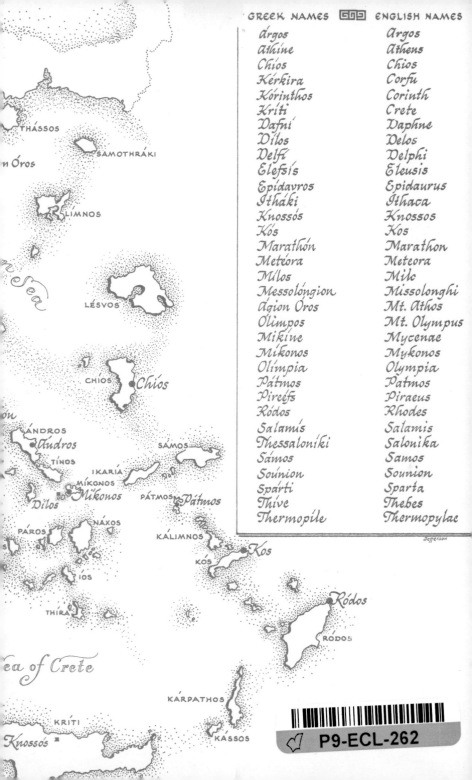

GREEK NAMES	ENGLISH NAMES
Árgos	Argos
Athíne	Athens
Chíos	Chios
Kérkira	Corfu
Kórinthos	Corinth
Kríti	Crete
Dafní	Daphne
Dílos	Delos
Delfí	Delphi
Elefsís	Eleusis
Epídavros	Epidaurus
Itháki	Ithaca
Knossós	Knossos
Kós	Kos
Marathón	Marathon
Metéora	Meteora
Mílos	Milo
Messolóngion	Missolonghi
Agion Óros	Mt. Athos
Olìmpos	Mt. Olympus
Mikíne	Mycenae
Míkonos	Mykonos
Olìmpia	Olympia
Pátmos	Patmos
Pireéfs	Piraeus
Ródos	Rhodes
Salamís	Salamis
Thessaloníki	Salonika
Sámos	Samos
Soúnion	Sounion
Spárti	Sparta
Thíve	Thebes
Thermopíle	Thermopylae

Jefferson

THÁSSOS
SAMOTHRÁKI
n Óros
LÍMNOS
n Sea
LÉSVOS
CHÍOS Chíos
ÁNDROS
Andros
SAMOS
TÍNOS
IKARÍA
MÍKONOS
Dílos Míkonos
PÁTMOS Pátmos
PÁROS
NÁXOS
KÁLIMNOS
ÍOS
KÓS Kos
THÍRA
Ródos
RÓDOS
ea of Crete
KÁRPATHOS
KRÍTI
Knossós
KÁSSOS

The Art of
GREEK COOKERY

BASED ON *THE GRECIAN GOURMET*

The Art of
GREEK COOKERY

BASED ON *THE GRECIAN GOURMET*

•

By the Women of
St. Paul's Greek Orthodox Church
Hempstead, Long Island, New York

DRAWINGS BY ART SEIDEN

•

DOUBLEDAY & COMPANY, INC.
GARDEN CITY, NEW YORK

CONTENTS

Words followed by an asterisk (*) are defined
in the Glossary in the back of this book.
Recipes for items shown in the text in small capital
letters can be found by consulting the Index.

FOREWORD

Glory be to our Heavenly Father for the wisdom, strength, and countless Blessings He has bestowed upon us. We praise His Holy Name for having enabled our Community of Saint Paul's to accomplish unbelievable strides and achievements in only ten years of Community history.

One of the greatest blessings of our beloved Community was the formation of the Saint Paul's Mr. and Mrs. Club, which has given nourishment to our Community and has given the necessary Christian fellowship to its members.

Contrary to the general opinion that "a committee is a group that keeps minutes and wastes time," the Mr. and Mrs. Club functions marvelously well through its various committees. One of these committees, composed of young housewives with great perseverance, has toiled almost with religious fervor over two years to bring forth this compilation of proven recipes for the general public.

We have seen many cookbooks. Perhaps some may meet the necessary high standards of culinary art. In this case, having closely followed the zeal of these women—their total disregard for time when it was necessary to prove a certain recipe—I believe that we have before us a cookbook which will excel in its field.

I have written many things in my life; in a way it did appear odd for me, a Priest in the Service of God, to write even a few lines for the foreword of a cookbook, since food belongs strictly to the material. However, I did this with great joy, knowing the spiritual bond it has cultivated amongst the Committee, and the fact that God has given us the right to enjoy bountiful blessings. Therefore, never let us forget the words of St. Paul to the Corinthians (1 Cor. 10:31): "Whether therefore ye eat, or drink, or whatsoever ye do, do all to the glory of God." When this becomes our measure in life everything becomes a true blessing.

Congratulations to each and every member of the Recipe Committee of the St. Paul's Mr. and Mrs. Club for a project noteworthy and well done.

FATHER GEORGE PAPADEAS,
Pastor, St. Paul's Greek Orthodox Church

THE RECIPE COMMITTEE

MRS. GEORGE ARAPAKIS

MRS. TOM BARBATSULY

MRS. GEORGE CALFO

MRS. THEODORE CARNAVOS

MRS. PETER CARPOU

MRS. JAMES CIDIS

MRS. WILLIAM DJINIS

MRS. GEORGE HAYES

MRS. JAMES KOLLAR

MRS. CHRIST LOUREKAS

MRS. CHARLES MARAVELL

MRS. GEORGE PAPADEAS

MRS. JAMES PAPPAS

MRS. MICHAEL POULOS

MRS. JAMES SKEADOS

MRS. LEE VLAHAKIS

NOTES

In 1951, the suburban village of Hempstead, New York, saw the birth of its first Greek Orthodox Church, namely St. Paul's, under the leadership of the Reverend Father George Papadeas. Two years later Father Papadeas organized the Mr. and Mrs. Club to provide a social organization for people of a common ethnic heritage. As the community grew so did the Mr. and Mrs. Club, until it became the center of many diversified and pleasurable activities, and special groups were created within the Club to further a closer relationship among members with mutual interests.

The Recipe Committee was one of these special groups of members with mutual culinary interests who met at monthly intervals at each other's homes to enjoy a social evening, to sample some special Greek dishes, and to exchange recipes.

In 1958, when a dream to construct a newer and larger church to accommodate the ever-increasing number of parishioners was realized, the Recipe Committee found further purpose for its existence, and that was to publish a cookbook to help with the erection and embellishment of the new edifice.

Recipes were assembled by the group itself, and culinary contributions were solicited among friends, relatives, and other members of the community. At the end of two and a half years of compiling, sorting, testing, editing, and finally printing, the first thesaurus of cherished Greek recipes was privately printed under the title of THE GRECIAN GOURMET, and all proceeds from the sale of this book, and from a second printing in 1962, were donated to the Building Fund of St. Paul's Greek Orthodox Church of Hempstead, New York.

Shortly after its publication, THE GRECIAN GOURMET captured the fancy of the food editors of both the New York *Herald Tribune* and the New York *Times*, and editorial spreads on the food pages of these newspapers praised the book and the Greek cuisine so vividly detailed in its pages. Letters and orders poured in from all over the country. People who had previously bought one copy ordered more—sometimes as many as a dozen—to give to their neighbors and friends. It became obvious that this was more than a book of recipes compiled by first-generation Greeks for the benefit of the future generations of Greek Americans. It was a book that had immense appeal for all food-conscious people; for gourmets and experimental cooks of all kinds; for tourists who, upon returning from Greece, wished to duplicate in their own kitchens some of the interesting and exciting dishes they had tasted in Greece and on the Grecian islands.

Shortly before Christmas, 1962, it was my pleasure to be the one to announce to members of the Mr. and Mrs. Club that a new and enlarged edition of THE GRECIAN GOURMET would be published by Doubleday & Company, Inc. in a handsome hard-cover and distributed throughout the world under the new title of THE ART OF GREEK COOKERY. This was something never anticipated, even in a dream, and I know I can speak for the entire Recipe Committee when I say thanks to all of you whose enthusiasm and praise of THE GRECIAN GOURMET made possible the publication of THE ART OF GREEK COOKERY.

And as our new church nears completion, we of the Recipe Committee feel more than compensated for the effort and time that the original project entailed. I can't say "work," for it was a work of love—and a great pleasure for all of us.

Again, our thanks.

THEODORA N. LOUREKAS,
Chairman of the Recipe Committee

PREFACE

It is not totally farfetched to say that the 1960s was the decade when America discovered Greece. Travelers by the thousands cruised Hellenic skies, sailed the Aegean, roamed the streets of Athens, Piraeus, and the sun-baked islands. Many, of course, returned with appetites whetted by that most excellent of Greek soups, the one called *avgolemono* made with rich chicken broth, egg yolks, and lemon. Many of them, too, must have hungered at length for stuffed vine leaves, for succulent lamb baked with artichokes, and for those honeyed desserts whose origins stretch back into antiquity.

Well, 1961 saw the first appearance of a small but engaging volume of recipes titled *The Grecian Gourmet*. It was compiled to produce funds for the St. Paul's Greek Orthodox Church of Hempstead, Long Island. In preparing the book a committee was formed to collect traditional recipes, which often required the advice and counsel of several grandmothers. A few recipes, nearly forgotten for a quarter of a century or more, were remembered and the results were admirable. It may well have been the best volume on Greek cooking yet written.

The book achieved a well-deserved fame to the great and understandable delight of the church congregation. And so, today, the volume has been revivified to its own greater glory. The present edition, with its proud new hard cover, lists fifty additional recipes, a section on feast days and holidays, an enlarged glossary, and chapters on Greek wines and traditional menus.

It is cordially recommended not only to travelers to the Isles of Greece, but for those inspired and adventurous cooks who want to know more about the world's most interesting cuisines.

CRAIG CLAIBORNE
April 17, 1963

INTRODUCTION

Greece, land of mythological romance and antiquity, bequeathed to the world not only its art and its architecture, but the art of dining and many of the basic principles of cooking.

To ancient Greece we owe the basic white sauce, invented by the kitchen sage Orion, and the basic brown sauce, formulated by Lampriadas. It was Agres of Rhodes who discovered how to fillet a fish, and Euthymus who created exquisite dishes of vegetables and salad greens. To the Greeks we owe the discovery of the oyster as an edible mollusk, the popularity of cabbage, the cultivation of the Egyptian onion, and the creation of the first pastry.

We have inherited a wealth of early writings about food from Greek philosophers and poets. Artemidorus made a collection of and commented on the culinary terms in use in his time. Timachildas was not only a poet but a cook who composed an epic on cooking, and Dionysius wrote of cooking and what, in his estimation, constituted the perfect cook. Then there was the philosopher Archestratus, who traveled far and wide in search of new delicacies to put upon his table and new ways to cook them. Many of the earliest recipes, written by him around 350 B.C., are still being used in Greece today.

The modern Greek inherited from the ancients not only his cuisine but his way of life, which still reflects a spirit of moderation mixed with a desire for perfection in all things. Moderation is evidenced in his leisurely pace of living and in the simplicity of his home, his clothes, and his buildings.

The day of a modern Greek is well balanced with work and pleasure. His afternoon siestas give him the opportunity to complete a working day with *glendi,* or a good time. He congregates with his friends at the local *tavernes,* or cafés, to discuss the problems of the day—economical, political, or religious—exchanging his ideas in the good-natured way that has been a national pastime since before the birth of Christ. Here in the *taverna* he sips a glass of ouzo or wine as he samples the various appetizers set before him—an assortment of cheese, olives, nuts, and pastries—for a Greek will not drink without eating. He has enjoyed wine since the beginning of time, and the present-day habit of the villagers of dipping bread into wine and olive oil represents the survival of an ancient custom.

The Greeks believe they have the finest grapes in the world and, therefore, the best wines. Perhaps the most controversial Greek wines are the retsinas, which, although the national beverage of Greece, are heavily flavored with resin, a taste for which must be acquired before the wine is enjoyed by most people. Once this taste is acquired, the retsinas can be a pleasantly different experience. The origin of these wines is interesting. Long before casks and bottles were invented, the Greeks aged their wines in goatskins and poured pitch-pine on top to preserve them. They developed a liking for the flavor of the pitch and continued to add resin to their wines after both casks and bottles were in common usage.

The motivation of the Greek's zest for good living—for good food and good wine—combined with his inherited characteristic for perfection has given Greece a culinary art of great distinction. It is an infinitely interesting cuisine, and little has been written of its intricacies and characteristic flavors. Recipes, for the most part, have been handed down from mother to daughter, from one generation to the next, without being formally recorded in a cookbook for modern Greek homemakers or for anyone else wishing to duplicate the dishes in his own kitchen. The ever-increasing number of visitors to Greece and the Greek islands return with haunting memories of delicate pastries, skewered lamb flavored with oregano and garlic, interesting casseroles, and delicious vegetables bathed in a rich golden sauce. They, as well as many American homemakers with an inquisitive palate and a desire to increase their repertoire of cooking, will find incredible pleasure in this book. The recipes are family recipes tested and perfected in American kitchens for American cooks. The ingredients, for the most part, are available in supermarkets throughout the country. For the few special Greek seasonings, for Greek cheese, fish roe, phyllo pastry sheets, and other Greek delicacies, we have included a list of markets in various key cities where these ingredients may be purchased.

All measurements given in the book are level measurements in standard measuring cups and spoons. In baking it goes without saying that the oven should always be preheated; the entree dishes serve from 4 to 6, depending on the size of one's appetite.

A word about phyllo (pronounced pheelo) pastry sheets.* These are available fresh at Greek bakeries and also frozen in the frozen food compartments of other specialty food outlets. The fresh ones freeze well and keep for a long time if well wrapped in moisture- and vapor-proof paper or aluminum foil. Phyllo pastry sheets are usually sold by the pound and there are many, many sheets per pound, for each is as thin as tissue paper. They are 12×18-inch rectangles and actually look like tissue paper. They dry out quickly, so must be kept constantly covered with a slightly dampened towel when not being used. Once American homemakers discover how easy it is to use phyllo sheets for hot cocktail hors d'oeuvres, for bottom and top layers of pies—both sweet and savory, and for rich and delicate pastries, we are sure that the production and distribution of them will be greatly increased. You will find many recipes using phyllo in the appetizer, entree, and dessert chapters of this book.

CUSTOMS AND TRADITIONS

The heart and soul of a country is reflected in its customs and traditions. And so it is with Greece, where the traditional ceremonies, the feasts and fast days of ancient origin, are closely associated with religion and portray the dominance of the Church in the life of every Greek Orthodox.

The first important event is the Baptism ceremony, at which three Sacraments are administered: Chrismation, Baptism, and Communion. The child is anointed with oil, as were the kings upon their coronation, symbolizing that he too is entering a new kingdom, the Kingdom of God. The oil symbolically prevents the devil from grasping the child as he foregoes all evil and adopts Christianity. His clothes are exchanged for new ones, a gift from the godfather to the new little Christian, and at the end of the ceremony the godfather passes *koufeta*, or Jordan almonds, to the guests, denoting a wish for nothing but sweetness in their lives.

The second important event in an individual's life is the wedding. The Greek Orthodox ceremony is a long one and, at the end, the couple feel they have been joined together for a lifetime. Double rings are blessed and exchanged. The couple sip wine from the same cup to signify the joy and bitterness they will share in life. Wreaths of orange blossoms are crossed three times over their heads, giving the blessings of the Holy Trinity to the new partnership, and, again, the *koufeta* are distributed to the guests.

The Greek people celebrate name days instead of birthdays. At baptism, each Greek Orthodox receives the name of a Christian Saint, who becomes his patron. On the day of the Saint's commemoration the namesake also celebrates. Preparations are made for open house. Special sweets, such as kourabiedes* and baklava,* are baked. Friends and relatives arrive to extend their wishes for "*Hronia Polla,*" which, literally translated, means "many years" and signifies their wishes for a long and happy life to the celebrant.

And, finally, the death of a Greek is mourned on memorial services held after forty days, at the end of one year, and at the end of three. The traditional kolyva,* a unique combination of cooked wheat, raisins, and pomegranate seeds, is made and brought to the Church to be blessed and distributed to the congregation. The wheat signifies everlasting life, the raisins represent sweetness, and the pomegranate seeds are symbolic of plenty.

The Greeks celebrate the New Year with the Feast of St. Basil. This is a family holiday and even the young children are allowed to stay up late to see the new year in. They congregate, young and old, and sing the *"Kalanda,"* carol-type songs to the patron Saint, who is known as the donor of wishes and blessings. The Vasilopeta,* or New Year's cake, is the highlight of the feast. The cake is blessed, cut, and served by the head of the household. The first piece is set aside for the Lord Jesus, the second for Our Lady Theotokos, the next for St. Basil, and subsequent pieces are served to each member of the family, beginning with the eldest. In one piece a silver or gold coin is hidden and great excitement prevails as each piece is cut to see who will find the coin and be the lucky one for the entire new year. Another custom is for the head of the house to break open a pomegranate on the doorstep of his home. If the fruit is full of seeds, the year will be a good, prosperous, and happy one. Gifts are exchanged on New Year's Day rather than on Christmas, in honor of St. Basil, the epitome of philanthropy, who developed for the needy a whole city, Basilias, which still bears his name.

Apokreos is a gay, festive time of parties and masquerades. It is the carnival that precedes the forty-day fast before Easter. Dinner on Palm Sunday features a variety of fish dishes, and the table is decorated with the palms received at the morning Liturgy. Holy Week follows, and preparations for Easter get under way. On Holy Thursday, the lambropsomo* (Easter bread) and the koulourakia* are baked. On Holy Thursday or Holy Saturday the eggs are dyed red to remind us that the blood of Christ redeemed the world. The egg, itself a symbol of the Resurrection, contains life motionless: in like manner, after a period of being motionless in the grave, we shall come forth with new life. On Good Friday nothing is done; the Greek Orthodox person is absorbed with the sufferings of our Lord. In commemoration of our Lord's being given vinegar mixed with bile when He asked for water, it is customary on Good Friday to eat lentil soup with vinegar.

After the Resurrection Liturgy early Easter morn, each family carries home the lighted candles and, on entering, pauses to form a candle-smoke cross near the top of the doorframe; this is allowed to remain throughout the year. The long fast is broken as the family sups on mageritsa,* *lambropsomo, koulourakia,* and Easter eggs. The eggs are cracked against each other by members of the family who say *"Christos Anesti"* [Christ is risen] and *"Alithos Anesti"* [Indeed He is risen]. The cracking of the eggs symbolizes the loosening of the bonds that held man captive, and now, in Christ, he is free. The greetings *"Christos Anesti"* and *"Alithos Anesti"* take the place of "good morning" or "good evening" among the Greek Orthodox people until Ascension Day. On Easter Sunday the yearling lamb is roasted on the spit, and joy and festivities resound throughout the country.

The Greek calendar is dotted with religious holidays, but the next major holiday is Christmas, the day that commemorates the birth of Christ. Roast lamb, turkey, or spit-roasted suckling pig are the favorite roasts set upon the lavish Christmas table, and christopsomo* and *kourabiedes* are served in every home.

In one section of this book we present a series of holiday menus, plus a few family menus for any day of the year, for anyone wishing to dine in the Greek manner.

The following chapter on feast days highlights the most important festivals of the Greek Orthodox Church.

FEAST DAYS

December 25 – THE NATIVITY OF OUR LORD AND SAVIOUR

Although the Greek Orthodox religious calendar commences September 1st, we shall begin explaining the twelve major feast days with the Nativity of our Lord, December 25th. The forty-day Fast of the Nativity begins on November 15th. During this time the Greek Orthodox communicant prepares spiritually and physically to receive the Sacrament of Holy Communion. Christmas Day is deeply felt; the hymns of the day are sung: "Christ is born, glorify Him; Christ came down from the Heavens, receive Him; Christ is on earth, arise even unto the Heavens. . . ." The day is strictly Christ-centered. All over Greece, in the cities as well as in the remote villages, children in small groups will knock on every door and offer to sing the carols, which, besides their religious content, express good wishes to the master and his household. In Greece gifts are exchanged on St. Basil's Day, January 1st, rather than on Christmas Day. Christmas is the beginning of a twelve-day festive period that ends with the Day of the Epiphany.

January 6th – EPIPHANY DAY

Epiphany Day, January 6th, a great day in the Greek Orthodox Church, commemorates Christ's baptism in the River Jordan. The celebrant priest blesses the water in the font with special prayers and sings the Baptismal Hymn as he immerses the cross in the Holy Water. He blesses the congregation and gives to each a vial of Holy Water to take home. A portion of this Holy Water is drunk after fasting and a little is sprinkled in each room of the home.

February 2d – HYPAPANTE CANDLEMAS

The fortieth-day blessing, which was a Hebrew custom, brought the Holy Mother to the Temple with the Christ child. There, the prophet Simeon received his Lord and blessed both. February 2d marks this day and is celebrated with a special Divine Liturgy. Since that time, each Greek Orthodox mother brings her infant to the Church forty days after birth to receive the blessings of God from the priest for herself and her child.

APOKREOS

Apokreos, the name given to the week preceding Lent, is a gay time of festivities, parties, and masquerades. The carnival begins with Meat Fare Sunday. On this day, and during the carnival week, all meat in the house is consumed or disposed of and, by the following Sunday, Cheese Fare Sunday, all the cheese, butter, and eggs are finished. The following day is Pure Monday, the first day of the long forty-day fast before the joyful Easter celebration. During this time no meat, fish, milk, butter, cheese, or eggs are eaten until Easter Sunday. The only exceptions are Annunciation Day and Palm Sunday, when the Church permits the eating of fish. The faithful discipline themselves with fasting and prayer and in doing so have the opportunity to become spiritually strong.

March 25th – THE ANNUNCIATION OF THE VIRGIN MARY

The Annunciation of the Virgin Mary, celebrated on March 25th, has a double significance for the Greek Orthodox people. The Divine Liturgy of the day commemorates the message of the Archangel Gabriel to the Virgin Mary: "Rejoice! Mary, full of grace; the Lord is with you: blessed are you among women." A Doxology follows the Liturgy as thanks and glorification to God for Greece's independence from the Ottoman Turks on this day in 1821. The Greeks were free for the first time since the fall of Constantinople in 1453. This holiday is always within the strict Lenten period, but because it is a festive day, the Church permits the eating of fish.

PALM SUNDAY

On the Sunday preceding Holy Week, we celebrate the entrance of our Lord into Jerusalem, when the multitudes laid down their garments for Jesus to pass over them and strewed His path with palm branches as they sang loudly: "Hosanna. Blessed is He Who cometh in the name of the Lord." Palms are distributed to the congregation after the Liturgy. On this day the Lenten fast is relieved, and the eating of fish is permitted.

HOLY WEEK

Each day during Holy Week, or the week of the Passion, the events of our Lord's life are relived. We suffer with Christ in order that we may be resurrected with Him. On Holy Thursday night excerpts of the Twelve Gospels are read relating Christ's Passion. The hearts of the faithful feel pain when the crucified Lord is taken in procession around the Church. Good Friday is such a great day of sorrow in the Greek Orthodox Church that it is the only day of the year when the Divine Liturgy may not be celebrated. In the morning we hear the Royal Hours and the Vesper services.

The body of Christ is taken down from the Cross, carried around the Church in the Holy Shroud, and then placed in the Sepulchre, the *Epitaphios,* to signify the burial of Christ. The *Epitaphios* is decked with many beautiful flowers. The faithful file past this symbolic Tomb. At the Lamentation service Friday evening, the priest and the choir chant the traditional Byzantine hymns around the *Epitaphios.*

EASTER SUNDAY

The Vesper services for Easter are held Saturday morning and are recognized as the preliminary to the Holy Resurrection. During the Divine Liturgy which follows, the priest throws laurel or bay leaves throughout the Church as a sign of joy that the Resurrection is at hand. He sings: "Arise O God and judge the earth, because You will win over all the nations."

Shortly before midnight on Holy Saturday the congregation gathers in the Church, each holding a candle, to await the Resurrection light from the Holy Altar. At midnight all lights, except the flame of the eternal vigil light, are extinguished. The priest lights his candle from the flame and exits from the Royal Altar Doors chanting, "Receive ye the light, from the light that never wanes, and glorify Christ who has risen from the dead." The light is transmitted to the candles held by the altar boys and then, one by one, to the whole congregation. Soon the dark church, which symbolizes the darkness of the grave, is brilliant with candlelight. At the end of the Liturgy, red-dyed eggs, symbolic of the Resurrection, are distributed, and the streets leading from the Church gradually become alive with hundreds of flickering lights as the congregation wend their way home.

The service on the afternoon of Easter Sunday is highlighted with the reading of the Resurrection Gospel in various languages to signify the universality of the Christian faith.

ASCENSION DAY

Ascension Day, the fortieth day after Easter, commemorates Christ's last appearance on earth. This final appearance was made before all of his disciples as they were gathered in Jerusalem with the Virgin Mary. A Divine Liturgy is held on this day.

PENTECOST SUNDAY

Pentecost, from a Greek word meaning "fiftieth," signifies the fiftieth day after Easter. On this day our Church commemorates the beginning of the Christian Church, when in Jerusalem three thousand people were baptized into Christianity. Special services are held to celebrate the descent of the Holy Spirit to the Apostles, as promised by the Lord.

August 6th – TRANSFIGURATION DAY

Transfiguration Day, August 6th, is the occasion when Christ manifested His heavenly glory to three of His apostles. On this day people bring to the Church the first fruits from their vineyards and orchards to be blessed and distributed to the congregation. Though August 6th falls during the Fast of the Virgin Mary, the eating of fish is permitted.

August 15th – THE ASSUMPTION OF THE VIRGIN MARY

The fifteen-day Fast of the Virgin Mary is in preparation for the Great Feast of the Assumption of the Virgin Mary. On this day the faithful receive Holy Communion. While the relics of many saints remain on earth, no relics remain of the Virgin Mary since her body was taken up into Heaven.

September 8th – THE NATIVITY OF THE THEOTOKOS

The daughter born to Joachim and Anna, named Mary, meaning "Sovereign Lady," was dedicated to the service of the Lord. The birth of Mary, who was to become the mother of Jesus, is one of the twelve important feast days of the Greek Orthodox Church. This day is commemorated as the Nativity of the Theotokos.

September 14th – ELEVATION OF THE PRECIOUS AND LIFE-GIVING CROSS

In the fourth century, St. Helena, mother of Constantine the Great, Emperor of Rome, desired to discover the whereabouts of the Precious Cross. Though in her eighties she journeyed to Jerusalem, and there, attracted to a particular hillock covered with a fragrant green herb, *vasiliko* [sweet basil], she found the true Cross. The Patriarch of Jerusalem, Makarios, raised the Cross aloft.

This important feast day is celebrated by the Greek Orthodox Church and the hymn chanted is: "We venerate Thy Holy Cross, O Master, and Thy Holy Resurrection we glorify." This is the only one of the twelve feast days that does not commemorate some occasion in the life of Christ or the Virgin Mary. It is a strict fast day.

November 21st – PRESENTATION OF THE HOLY THEOTOKOS

Joachim and Anna had promised to dedicate their child to the Lord. When Mary was three years old, they led their daughter to the Temple in Jerusalem. Mary's entrance into the Temple, the Presentation of the Holy Theotokos, is one of the important feast days of the Greek Orthodox Church.

The customs attached to the traditional religious life offer a plan to make man worthy of his heavenly destination. Let us always remember that "the earth is the Lord's, and all the things therein; the world, and all those that reside therein."

MENUS

New Year's Dinner

Caviar Canapés   Taramasalata   Keftaidakia
Tiropetes   Spanakopetes   Rengha   Lakertha
Marinated Lamb Brains
Dolmadakia me Avgolemono
Roast Leg of Lamb

OR

Roast Stuffed Turkey
Potatoes   Greek Salad   Greek Bread
Feta   Kasseri   Mizithra   Calamata Olives   Radishes
Pepper Toursi
Vasilopeta
Kourabiedes   Fenikia   Skaltsonakia
Fruit   Almonds   Walnuts   Filberts   Dried Fruit
Kydoni Xysto
Greek Coffee

Meat Fare Sunday

Keftaidakia   Bourekakia me Kreas   Tiropetes
Yogurt Dip   Baked Lamb Brains   Anchovy Canapés
Roast Leg of Lamb
Pastichio   String Beans   Greek Salad   Crusty Bread
Galatoboureko   Kourabiedes   Trigona   Ravani
Greek Coffee

Cheese Fare Sunday

Shrimp with Mayonnaise Sauce   Caviar Canapés
Anchovy Canapés
Dolmadakia Yialandji   Stuffed Mussels   Pickled Squid
Cheese Balls   Yogurt Dip   Fried Kasseri
Tiropeta   Spanakopeta
Stuffed Tomatoes   Greek Salad   Feta   Kasseri   Mizithra
Copenhagen   Kourabiedes   Nut Turnovers   Karidata
Greek Coffee

Palm Sunday

Shrimp with Lemon Slices   Taramasalata
Fish Soup Avgolemono
Boiled Fish with Oil and Lemon Sauce

OR

Fish Plaki
Fried Fish with Skordalia Sauce   Imam Baildi
Greek Salad   Calamata Olives   Pepper Toursi   Greek Bread
Fruit   Halva
Greek Coffee

Easter Dinner

Lamb Liver Meze   Marinated Lamb Brains   Lamb Heads
Mageritsa
Artichokes Politika
Kokoretsi Souvlakia
Spit-Roasted Baby Lamb
Potatoes or Pastichio
Lambropsomo with Red Eggs
Celery   Radishes   Calamata Olives   Feta   Kasseri   Mizithra
Tsoureki
Red Eggs
Kourabiedes   Koulourakia   Baklava
Greek Coffee

Christmas Dinner

Slivers of Pork Simmered in Wine

Loukanika   Lamb Liver Meze   Bourekakia me Kreas

Tiropetes   Lakertha   Sardines   Anchovies

Moussaka

and

Roast Leg of Lamb with Potatoes

OR

Chicken Soup Avgolemono

and

Roast Turkey Stuffed with Chestnuts

and

Potatoes

OR

Sarmades

and

Spit-Roasted Suckling Pig

Calamata Olives   Feta   Kasseri   Mizithra   Pepper Toursi

Radishes

Greek Salad   Christopsomo

Kourabiedes   Fenikia   Baklava   Floyeres

Quince Pelte   Dried Figs Stuffed with Nuts   Dates

Roasted Chestnuts   White Raisins   Stragalia and Salted Stragalia

Greek Coffee

Party Menu I

Taramasalata   Keftaidakia   Lamb Liver Meze
Tiropetes   Spanakopetes
Avgolemono Soup
Roast Leg of Lamb with Artichokes
Potatoes   String Bean Salad   Greek Salad
Greek Bread
Apricot Chocolate Custard Cake
Greek Coffee

Party Menu II

Anchovy Canapés   Yogurt Dip   Marinated Cocktail Meatballs
Rengha   Pepper Salad
Roast Leg of Lamb
Pastichio   Baked Zucchini
Greek Salad   Greek Olives   Feta Cheese
Greek Bread
Baklava
Greek Coffee

Party Menu III

Sardine Canapés   Eggplant Dip   Loukanika
Tiropetes   Baked Lamb Brains
Roast Loin of Pork
Artichokes with Fava Beans   Potatoes
Beet Salad   Greek Bread
Ravani
Greek Coffee

Barbecue Menu I

Caviar Canapés   Keftaidakia   Dolmadakia   Tiropetes
Bourekakia me Kreas
Shish Kebab
Rice Pilaf   Imam Baildi
Greek Salad   Greek Bread
Baklava
Greek Coffee

Barbecue Menu II

Dolmadakia   Lamb Liver Meze   Keftaidakia   Tsiri
Spanakopetes
Broiled Chicken
Rice Pilaf   Broccoli with Oil and Lemon Sauce
Greek Salad   Greek Bread
Rum Cake à la Grecque
Greek Coffee

Buffet Supper Menu I

Taramasalata   Keftaidakia   Tiropetes   Feta Cheese   Kasseri
Greek Olives
Moussaka
Stuffed Tomatoes Laderes
Greek Salad   Greek Bread
Copenhagen
Greek Coffee

Buffet Supper Menu II

Taramasalata   Keftaidakia   Tiropetes   Feta Cheese   Kasseri
Greek Olives
Pastichio
Eggplant Salad   String Beans with Oil and Lemon Sauce
Greek Bread
Galatoboureko
Greek Coffee

Buffet Supper Menu III

Keftaidakia   Tiropetes   Spanakopetes   Lamb Liver Meze
Dolmadakia me Avgolemono
Greek Salad   Greek Bread
Almond Torte
Greek Coffee

Family Menus

Family dinners are simple and usually consist of a main dish, salad, crusty bread, a simple dessert, and milk or coffee. The following nourishing, simple-to-prepare Greek dishes are the favorites:

Lamb Stew with Vegetable   Mussels with Rice

Chicken Pilaf   Chicken Stefado

Chicken with Dill Sauce   Giouvetsi

Fish Plaki   Meat Balls à la Smyrna

The favorite family desserts are:
Rizogalo, Krema Karamela, Apple Compote, Yogurt, and Fresh Fruit and Cheese.

GREEK WINES

Dionysus (Bacchus) in Greek mythology was originally a nature god of fruitfulness and vegetation, especially of the vine—thus, the god of wine. The Greeks, then, have had an intimate kinship with the products of the vine since ancient times, and wine is a constant companion at mealtime for all socioeconomic levels.

Greek wines cover a broad spectrum. The wine industry is just beginning to channel a representative variety to the export market. Blessed with the Mediterranean sun and dry, mountainous slopes, Greece is preoccupied with the vine and its by-products. Local pride runs high, and the Greeks love to point out that other nations of the Continent buy Greek wines and brandies to blend and fortify their products.

As a rule, the Greek is not a meticulous follower of wine etiquette as it concerns use of the "proper" wine with each course. He often prefers to stay with his "favorite," be it white, rosé, or red, for all courses. And most of the Greek wines, in large measure due to climate and diet, lean to the "light" side of the spectrum. A convenient breakdown of types and names of wines now being exported to the U.S.A. follows:

WHITE (serve chilled)

St. Helena – an aristocratic wine often gracing the table at formal state dinners

Demestica – light and very fine

Robola – a specialty from the island of Samos (not too dry)

Aphrodite – a dry vintage wine from Cyprus

Hymettus – round, dry, from the mountain area giving Greece's best honey

Retsina – the famous resin-flavored wine of the people. The uninitiated often have to acquire a taste for it

ROSÉ'S (serve chilled or at room temperature)

Roditys – light, dry, popular all-purpose wine

Kokineli – full-bodied companion to Retsina, resin-flavored

RED (serve at room temperature)
Castel Danielis – one of Greece's finest red wines
Pendeli – a fruity young wine, light
Mt. Ambelos – full-bodied, smooth
Claret – a Cyprus wine of repute
Othello – heavy, velvety contender from Cyprus

Greece is widely respected for a number of "specialties" in the area of sweet wines, liqueurs, and brandies. The most important are:

DESSERT WINES
Mavrodaphne
Comanderie St. John (1927 vintage)
Commandaria KEO
Muscat-Samos

LIQUEURS
Metaxa (5 and 7 stars) – liqueur brandy
Achaia-Clauss (5 stars) – liqueur brandy
Mastiha – anise-flavored, favored by the ladies

BRANDIES
Cambas – VO, 25 years old
VSOP, 30 years old
KEO – 12 years old

MISCELLANEOUS
Ouzo – darling of the sidewalk café crowd. A potent, colorless distillation from grape mash, running as high as 100 proof. Lightly flavored with anise (like the French Pernod), and a real "cooler" on the rocks.

Finding all these may take some shopping, even in the finer liquor stores. A New York City source is the Athens Liquor Store, 300 West Fortieth Street (opposite the Port Authority Bus Terminal just off Eighth Avenue).

Greek wines recommended to accompany main courses of suggested Greek dinners:

DINNER	WINES	SOME FINE BRANDS
ROAST LAMB	*Roditys*	*Achaia-Clauss; Cambas; Marko; Evi-Evan*
	Pendeli	*Cambas*
	Retsina	*Cambas*
SUCKLING PIG	*St. Helena*	*Achaia-Clauss*
or	*Demestica*	*Achaia-Clauss*
STUFFED TURKEY	*Retsina*	*Cambas*
	Robola	*EOS; Nicolaou*
	Aphrodite	*KEO*
	Hymettus	*Cambas*
	Roditys	*Achaia-Clauss; Cambas; Marko; Evi-Evan*

The Art of
GREEK COOKERY

BASED ON *THE GRECIAN GOURMET*

APPETIZERS

APPETIZERS

Appetizers are an important segment of Greek cooking and in them is reflected the Greek's love for a leisurely and friendly hour of socializing before the late dinner is served.

The Taverna, which plays an important part in the life of a Greek, gradually comes to life as the day draws to an end. Here the fun-loving Greeks gather with their friends to savor a variety of appetizers of cheese, olives, and sea food, and to laugh, sing, or solve the problems of the world over a glass, or many glasses, of ouzo* before wending their merry way home to dinner. Ouzo is an aromatic spirit derived from grapes, flavored with aniseed. It is a potent drink and most tourists in Greece will mix it with water, much to the dismay of the Greek, who drinks it plain or with ice. Some Greeks will forego the fiery ouzo in preference for a glass of Greek wine, distilled from a variety of grapes grown in the many vineyards throughout Greece. Two of the most popular of these are retsina* and mavrodaphne,* and are available at many large liquor stores throughout this country. Wine is indispensable at the table of the Greeks and anyone reproducing a Greek meal in his own home or serving a selection of Greek appetizers should be authentically Grecian and serve a Greek wine or ouzo.

Greek appetizers are called mezethakia* or orektika,* both words meaning "something to whet the appetite." In general, they are small, savory, and rich and, when consumed in reasonable quantities, do exactly that—whet the appetite. However, when someone being introduced for the first time to Greek cooking samples tiropetes,* tiny appetizers of feta cheese* wrapped in many layers of the most delicate, flaky pastry the world knows, or some of the other following delicious appetizers, he is apt to forget the true meaning of the word to the extent that dinner must be postponed indefinitely.

CANAPES, DIPS, AND HORS D'OEUVRES

CAVIAR CANAPE *Haviari Kanape*

Toast rounds or triangles
Butter
Black or red caviar

Lemon juice
Onion, finely chopped
Grated hard-cooked egg yolk

Cut toast in desired shapes; butter. Spread generously with caviar. Sprinkle with a little lemon juice and garnish with onion and egg yolk. Serve.

SARDINE CANAPE *Sardeles Kanape*

Sardines, canned boned
2 tablespoons softened butter

1 teaspoon lemon juice
Buttered bread rounds or crackers

Drain sardines and mash. Add softened butter and lemon juice; blend. Spread sardine paste on buttered bread rounds or crackers. Serve.

ANCHOVY CANAPE *Fileto Sardeles*

Toast strips or crackers
Cream cheese

Anchovy fillets
Capers (optional)

Spread strips of toast or crackers generously with cream cheese. Place an anchovy fillet on each. Garnish with capers if desired. Serve.

YOGURT DIP *Yiaourti Skordalia*

1 clove garlic
2 or 3 walnuts
1 teaspoon olive oil
1 cup yogurt

Salt and pepper to taste
Dash of vinegar (optional)
Diced cucumber

Mash garlic and walnuts with olive oil. Add mixture to yogurt. Add remaining ingredients. Chill. Serve as a dip with crackers. *Yield: 1 cup*

FISH ROE DIP   *Taramasalata*

⅓ of 8-ounce jar *tarama**	4 or 5 slices white bread,
1 small onion, finely grated	trimmed
1 or 2 cups olive oil	2 or 3 lemons, juice of

Mash *tarama* and add grated onion. Add a little of the olive oil and beat thoroughly to a smooth paste. Moisten bread and squeeze out excess water. Continue beating *tarama* mixture, adding alternately small bits of moistened bread, olive oil, and lemon juice. *Taramasalata* should be beaten until cream-colored. Serve as a dip with crackers or spread on toast. *Yield: 1½–2 cups*

Note: Any leftover *taramasalata* may be used as dressing for tossed salad.

EGGPLANT DIP   *Imam Baildi Meze*

1 recipe IMAM BAILDI
5 or 6 green olives, sliced
1 tablespoon capers

Follow recipe for *Imam Baildi*, using small eggplant as directed. Cool. Chop eggplant and add sliced olives and capers. Serve with crackers. *Yield: 1 cup*

COCKTAIL MEATBALLS   *Keftaidakia*

1 pound ground round steak	1 or 2 slices white bread
1 onion, finely grated	½ cup dry wine or water
1 or 2 cloves garlic, crushed	1 egg
Salt and pepper	Flour
Oregano	Olive oil
Mint	Butter

Mix meat, onion, garlic, salt, pepper, oregano, and mint. Remove crusts from bread slices and moisten in wine or water. Add bread and egg to meat. Knead mixture. Shape into 1-inch balls, dust with flour, and sauté in equal amounts of olive oil and butter. When meatballs are cooked and browned on all sides, place immediately in covered casserole and keep warm until ready to serve. *Yield: 1½–2 dozen*

MARINATED COCKTAIL MEATBALLS   *Keftaidakia me Saltsa*

1¼ pounds chopped beef
½ cup bread crumbs
1 egg
¼ cup water
1 teaspoon prepared mustard
1 tablespoon parsley flakes
Pinch oregano
1 grated onion
Garlic salt

Salt and pepper
1 teaspoon dried mint
1 teaspoon Worcestershire
  sauce
Dash allspice, cinnamon, and
  cloves
½ cup tomato sauce
¼ cup water

Mix all ingredients except tomato sauce and ¼ cup water and shape into 1-inch balls. Put on lightly greased baking pan and bake in a 450-degree oven for 20 minutes. Drain on absorbent paper. In a saucepan simmer tomato sauce and remaining water for 5 minutes. Correct seasoning. Add meatballs to sauce and allow to marinate overnight. Heat in covered casserole and serve hot. *Yield: 2–2½ dozen*

GREEK SAUSAGES   *Loukanika*

1 pound chopped beef
1 pound chopped pork
1 teaspoon crushed garlic
1 teaspoon cinnamon
1 teaspoon black pepper
1 teaspoon allspice

Thin orange rind of 1 orange,
  finely chopped
10–20 whole black peppercorns,
  cracked
4 ounces wine (½ cup)
Lemon juice

Mix all ingredients except lemon juice and marinate for one week in the refrigerator, stirring every day. Fry one small portion to check seasoning and, if necessary, add salt. Using proper attachment on meat grinder for stuffing, stuff mixture into casings separated into 12-inch lengths. Prick casings with fork. String stuffed casings up to dry, either in cold cellar or out-of-doors in cold weather in a protected area, for one week. Cut in 1-inch pieces and broil. Sprinkle with lemon juice and serve warm. *Yield: 2–2½ dozen*
Note: Casings may be purchased in pork stores.

LAMB LIVER MEZE *Sikotaki Meze*

>   1 pound lamb's liver   Dill, finely chopped
>   ¼ cup olive oil   1 lemon, juice of
>   1 bunch scallions, thinly sliced

Cut liver in bite-size pieces. Dip in boiling water and remove immediately. Fry quickly in olive oil until cooked, and remove to warm platter. Do not overcook. To oil remaining in pan add scallions and dill. Stir until scallions are soft and pour over liver with oil from pan. Sprinkle with lemon juice and additional chopped dill. Serve hot. *Yield: 2 dozen*

MARINATED LAMB BRAINS WITH LEMON SAUCE *Miala me Lemoni*

Wash brains thoroughly. Soak in lukewarm water for 10 minutes. With a sharp knife remove membranes. Rinse. Place brains in boiling water to cover, add 2 to 3 tablespoons vinegar, and simmer for 25 to 30 minutes or until soft. Drain. Cut in ½-inch cubes. Cool. Add lemon juice, olive oil (using proportions of 1 part lemon juice to 3 parts olive oil), salt, pepper, and finely chopped dill. Allow brains to marinate in sauce. Serve cold.

LAMB BRAINS, SAUTEED *Miala Tighanita*

Prepare and cook brains as above. Cut in 1-inch pieces and add salt and pepper. Dust lightly with flour and sauté in butter until lightly browned. Sprinkle with lemon juice and serve warm.

LAMB BRAINS, BAKED *Miala tou Fournou*

Wash brains thoroughly. Soak in lukewarm water for 10 minutes. With a sharp knife remove membranes. Rinse. Cut brains in half. Place in a shallow pan and sprinkle with lemon juice, olive oil, salt, pepper, and oregano. Bake in moderate 350-degree oven 1 hour until golden brown and soft. Serve hot or cold.

FRIED MUSSELS *Midia Tighanita*

Clean mussels thoroughly and pry open. Remove mussel meat and roll lightly in flour. Sauté in olive oil until lightly browned. Serve hot with GARLIC SAUCE.

FISH ROE PATTIES *Taramokeftaides*

2 pounds potatoes	Parsley, chopped
½ pound tarama*	Flour
1 or 2 scallions or leeks, chopped	Fat for frying (optional)

Boil potatoes in jackets until tender. Peel and mash. Add *tarama* to hot potatoes. Add scallions or leeks and parsley. Shape into small patties, roll in flour and fry in hot deep fat or broil on oiled shallow pan. Serve hot or cold. *Yield: 2 dozen*

Note: Larger-sized patties may be served for a luncheon or supper dish.

DRIED SALTED SMELTS *Tsiri*

Dip *tsiri* in a vinegar-water solution and dry on towel. Cook over hot coals in a barbecue pit until well browned. (*Tsiri* may be cooked in broiler.) Pound with a hammer until *tsiri* are soft and split in lengthwise pieces. Marinate in vinegar, olive oil, and pepper. To serve, arrange on serving dish, sprinkle with a little of the marinade, and garnish with finely chopped dill.

DRIED SMOKED HERRING *Rengha*

½ lemon, juice of
3 tablespoons olive oil
1 package dried, smoked, boned
herring

Beat lemon juice and olive oil until blended. Cut herring in small pieces and marinate in lemon juice and olive oil. Serve herring pieces on squares of toast or crackers. *8 servings*

CHEESE BALLS *Tirokeftaidakia*

1 egg white
2 cups Parmesan cheese, grated
Fat for frying

Beat egg white until stiff. To ⅔ of stiffly beaten egg white add 1 cup cheese and beat. Add remaining egg white and cheese alternately, beating constantly until thoroughly mixed. Shape into balls the size of small marbles and fry in hot deep fat (365 degrees) until golden. Drain on absorbent paper and serve warm. *Yield: 3 dozen*

FRIED CHEESE *Kasseri Tighanito*

The cheese used for this recipe should be kasseri,* kefalotiri,* or feta.* Cut cheese in slices ¼ inch thick and brown in butter. Sprinkle with lemon juice. Cut in bite-size pieces and serve immediately.

STUFFED GRAPEVINE LEAVES *Dolmadakia Yialandji*

4 medium onions, finely
chopped
1 teaspoon salt
⅔ cup raw rice
¾ cup olive oil
1 teaspoon mint, chopped
1 teaspoon fresh dill, chopped
½ cup parsley, chopped (reserve
stalks)

3 large bunches scallions including green, chopped
Salt and pepper
1 lemon, juice of
12 ounce jar grapevine leaves
Parsley stalks
1 cup boiling water
Additional lemon juice

Steam onions over very low heat with 1 teaspoon salt, stirring occasionally, for 5 to 10 minutes. Remove from heat. Add rice and ½ cup of the olive oil and mix. Add herbs and vegetables and mix. Add salt and pepper and half the lemon juice. Wash grapevine leaves thoroughly to remove all brine. Separate leaves carefully. Remove thick stem portions. Cut large leaves in half. Place 1 tablespoon filling on underside of leaf. Starting at base, fold over, and fold in sides, rolling tightly toward point.

Interlace parsley stalks on bottom of saucepan. Arrange *dolmadakia* in layers. Add the remaining oil and lemon juice. Weigh down *dolmadakia* with a heavy plate. Cover saucepan and simmer for 20 minutes over low heat. Add boiling water and simmer for 25 minutes longer. Serve cold, sprinkled with lemon juice. *Yield: 3 dozen*

Note: If desired, water may be added with oil to *dolmadakia*; allow the water to reach just above the level of the plate. Bring *dolmadakia* to boil quickly, lower flame, and simmer 45 minutes. Add juice of ½ lemon when done. Serve cold.

STUFFED MUSSELS   *Midia Yemista*

24 fresh mussels	½ cup raw rice
Salt	1 teaspoon allspice
1 cup water	¼ cup pignolia nuts
½ cup dry white wine	¼ cup currants
2 large onions, chopped	Black pepper to taste
¼ cup olive oil	2 tablespoons parsley, chopped

Remove beard from mussels and scrub shells well with hard brush under cold running water. Place them in a kettle, sprinkle with salt, and pour water and wine over them. Cover and steam for 10 minutes until shells open. Discard any shells that do not open.

In a separate pan, cook onions in olive oil until soft. Add rice and cook 3 minutes longer, stirring constantly. Add 1 cup of liquid drained from mussels and cook rice, covered, for 15 minutes. Add remaining ingredients, cover, and cook 5 minutes longer or until rice is done. Remove mussels from shells, add to rice, and cook over low heat until mussels are heated through. Fill mussel shells with mixture. Serve hot or cold. *Yield: 2 dozen*

STUFFED CUCUMBER   *Angouria Yemista*

Peel a cucumber and slice in half lengthwise. Scoop out seeds. Stuff with filling, such as chopped shrimp, lobster, or crab meat mixed with mayonnaise, or cream cheese mixed with feta cheese.* Chill well and serve sliced in bite-size pieces.

PEPPER SALAD APPETIZER   *Piperies Orektiko*

6 *large sweet peppers*	3 *tablespoons vinegar (more if*
1 *medium onion, coarsely*	*desired)*
chopped	¼ *cup olive oil*
Salt and pepper to taste	*Oregano*

Bake peppers in hot 450-degree oven for about 20 minutes or until wilted and soft. Remove seeds and outer skin. Cut in pieces and place in a bowl. Add onion, salt, and pepper. Mix vinegar and olive oil and add to peppers. Sprinkle with oregano. Adjust seasonings if necessary. Serve as appetizer. *12 servings*

PICKLED SQUID   *Kalamaria Toursi*

2 *pounds squid*	1 *teaspoon pickling spices tied*
2 *tablespoons olive oil*	*in cheesecloth*
¾ *cup vinegar*	*Salt and pepper to taste*

Wash and clean squid well and drain. Place in casserole (no water is necessary), cover, and cook for 30 minutes or until tender. Drain and chop, reserving the liquid for making *pilaf*. To squid in casserole add olive oil, vinegar, spices, and salt and pepper. Bring to a boil and simmer for 5 minutes. Discard spice bag. Transfer to bowl or jar and chill. Serve cold. *8 servings*

VEGETABLES IN BRINE   *Toursi*

Brine	*per quart jar:*
Whole green tomatoes	*Vinegar*
Celery stalks, in 2–3 inch pieces	2–3 *cloves garlic, halved*
Cauliflower	1 *teaspoon mixed whole spices*
Green peppers	1 *sprig dill*
Carrot sticks	

To make brine, insert a raw egg, in shell, in water, and add enough salt to water so that egg will break surface of water in the visible diameter of a dime. Wash all vegetables and place in quart jars. Fill jars with brine, sealing tightly. Shake and turn jars every other day for 10 days. Remove brine. Fill jars with vinegar. To each jar add garlic, mixed whole spices, and fresh dill.

Leave *toursi* in jars for 2 to 3 weeks, shaking now and then.

PHYLLO PASTRY RECIPES

The following recipes use phyllo pastry.* These recipes make excellent appetizers, if the portions are made small. However, any of these recipes may be adapted to luncheon or supper dishes by enlarging the size of the individual portion, or by making the recipe in a shallow pan and cutting in squares after baking. For pan method see recipe for SPINACH SQUARES (*Spanakopeta*).

CHEESE PUFFS   *Tiropetes*

1 pound feta cheese*
12-ounce package pot cheese
5 eggs
½ cup parsley or dill, finely chopped

½ pound butter (half margarine may be used)
1 pound phyllo pastry sheets

Crumble *feta* cheese into small pieces. Add pot cheese and blend well. Add eggs and beat thoroughly. Mix in the parsley or dill.

Melt butter. Carefully cut phyllo pastry into 3 equal portions. Refrigerate two-thirds until needed and cover the remaining third with a slightly dampened towel. Remove one sheet of phyllo pastry, place on a flat surface, and butter well. Fold in the long sides towards the middle, making a strip about 2 inches wide; butter again. Place one tablespoon of cheese mixture in the bottom right-hand corner of strip and fold over into triangle shape. Continue folding, making sure, with each fold, that the bottom edge is parallel with the alternate side edge. Lightly butter finished triangle. Continue in this manner until all the cheese and/or phyllo sheets are used.

Bake triangle puffs in a 425-degree oven for 20 minutes or until golden-browned, turning once. Allow to cool about 5 minutes before serving. Serve warm. *Yield: 75 pieces*

CHEESE TRIANGLES *Tiropetes*

12 tablespoons butter (¾ cup)
3 tablespoons flour
1½ cups milk
¾ pound feta cheese,* crumbled

Pepper
2 eggs plus 1 egg yolk
½ pound phyllo pastry sheets

In a saucepan melt half the butter. Add flour and stir until mixture becomes light brown. Remove from heat and slowly stir in hot milk. Cook, stirring constantly, until sauce is smooth and thickened. Add crumbled cheese and pepper and stir. Add eggs and egg yolk, one at a time, beating well after each addition.

Melt remaining butter. Cut sheets of phyllo pastry in 3-inch strips and spread with butter. Put one teaspoonful of cheese filling on end of strip, then fold into triangles as instructed in recipe for CHEESE PUFFS. After all the *tiropetes* are folded and ready, place on a baking pan and spread more butter on the top of each one. Bake in a 400-degree oven for 10 to 15 minutes until golden. Serve hot. *Yield: 60 pieces*

CHEESE TRIANGLES *Tiropitakia*

3 tablespoons butter
4 tablespoons flour
1 cup milk
½ pound feta cheese,* crumbled
3 ounces kefalotiri* or Guyère, grated
2 eggs, beaten

1 tablespoon parsley, finely chopped
¼ teaspoon nutmeg
⅛ teaspoon pepper
Melted butter
½ pound phyllo pastry sheets

Melt the 3 tablespoons of butter, add flour, and stir. When mixture starts to bubble, remove from heat and gradually stir in milk. Cook, stirring constantly, until smooth and thickened. Empty sauce into bowl, add cheese, eggs, parsley, and seasonings. Mix well. With melted butter and phyllo sheets, prepare triangles according to instructions given in recipe for CHEESE PUFFS. Bake in a 425-degree oven for about 20 minutes or until golden brown. Serve warm. *Yield: 40 pieces*

CHEESE PIE   *Tiropeta*

12 eggs	*½ pound phyllo pastry sheets*
1 pound feta cheese*	*½ pound butter, melted, for*
1 pound ricotta cheese	*buttering pastry*
½ pound butter, melted and	
cooled	

Beat eggs until thick. In another bowl mix cheese with ½ pound melted butter. Add eggs to cheese mixture. Line an 11×14×2-inch pan with 10 buttered sheets of phyllo pastry. Add egg-cheese mixture. Top with 8 buttered sheets of phyllo pastry. Do not cut. Bake in a 350-degree oven for about 30 minutes or until golden brown. Cut in squares. Serve warm. *Yield: 16 squares*

SPINACH CHEESE PUFFS   *Spanakopetes*

1 medium onion, finely chopped	*6 ounces pot cheese*
¼ cup olive oil	*3 eggs, beaten*
1 package frozen chopped	*¼ cup bread crumbs*
spinach, thawed, or 1 pound	*½ pound phyllo pastry sheets*
spinach, well washed and	*½ cup (¼ pound) butter, melted*
finely chopped	*(half margarine may be used)*
½ pound feta cheese*	

Sauté onion in olive oil for 5 minutes. Add spinach, from which as much water as possible has been drained. Simmer with the onion over a low flame, stirring occasionally, until most of moisture is evaporated.

Crumble *feta* cheese into small pieces. Add pot cheese and blend well. Add beaten eggs and mix well. Toss bread crumbs into spinach-onion mixture and add to cheese. Stir until well blended.

With buttered phyllo sheets, make the triangle puffs as instructed in recipe for CHEESE PUFFS. If spinach rolls are preferred, cut the sheets of phyllo pastry into quarters. Refrigerate 3 quarters, and cover the 1 quarter with a lightly dampened towel. Brush each quarter sheet well with melted butter. Place 1 tablespoon of the spinach cheese 1 inch from narrow edge of sheet. Fold the inch margin over mixture; fold long edges in toward middle. Butter again and roll compactly to end.

Bake the *spanakopetes* in a 425-degree oven for 20 minutes or until golden-browned, turning once. Allow to cool about 5 minutes before serving. Serve warm. *Yield: 40–50 pieces*

Note: This recipe may be made with American pie dough in a piepan. Serve in pie wedges.

SPINACH ROLLS   *Bourekia me Spanaki*

2 pounds spinach	Dash of pepper
1 ball mozarella cheese	Dash of cinnamon
1 cup grated Romano cheese	½ pound phyllo pastry sheets
4 tablespoons butter, diced	Melted butter
Pinch of salt	

Wash spinach well, drain, and dry thoroughly on paper toweling. Cut into small pieces. Dice *mozarella* cheese. Add to spinach along with the Romano, butter, salt, pepper, and cinnamon. Mix well.

Brush two sheets of phyllo pastry with melted butter, and place one on top of the other. Place a band of the spinach mixture lengthwise along one side of the sheets to within 2 inches of each end. Turn in the ends, roll lengthwise, and continue folding over until a long roll is formed. Brush roll with melted butter. Continue in this manner until all of the spinach mixture is used. Bake rolls in a 400-degree oven about 25 minutes or until golden-browned. Cut diagonally in 2-inch pieces. Serve warm. *Yield: 40 pieces*

SPINACH-CHEESE PASTRIES   *Spanakopetes*

Pastry Dough:

½ pound soft cream cheese
1 cup soft salted butter
2 cups sifted flour

Filling:

1 onion, finely chopped
3 tablespoons olive oil
1 package frozen chopped
   spinach, thawed and well
   drained
1 teaspoon salt
¼ pound feta cheese,* crumbled
4 ounces pot cheese
1 egg, beaten

To make the pastry dough: With a fork combine cream cheese and softened butter. Cut in the flour. Work with hands until dough holds together. Place on waxed paper, form into ball, and chill overnight. Roll out dough ⅛ inch thick with floured rolling pin on a generously floured surface. Cut in rounds with 1½- to 2-inch cutter.

To make filling: Sauté onion in olive oil until softened; add spinach and salt. Cook over low heat until tender. Mix cheese together and stir in egg. Add spinach-onion mixture and blend well. (Any leftover spinach-cheese mixture may be used in an omelet.)

Place a little spinach filling on each round and fold over. Moisten edge so it will hold together. Flute edge with a fork and prick center. Place pastries on a cooky sheet and bake in a 425-degree oven for 15 minutes, or until golden brown. Serve warm. *Yield: about 100 small pastries*

The pastries may be frozen before baking.

SPINACH SQUARES *Spanakopeta*

2 pounds spinach
1 onion, finely chopped
4 tablespoons butter
1 cup CREAM SAUCE
5 or 6 eggs, beaten

1 cup finely crumbled feta
  cheese*
Salt and pepper
Dash of nutmeg
½ pound phyllo pastry sheets
Melted butter

Wash spinach and discard stems. Dry as thoroughly as possible on absorbent paper and cut in pieces. Sauté onion in butter until soft. Add spinach and sauté a few minutes longer. Cool. Add cream sauce, eggs, cheese, salt, pepper, and nutmeg. Mix well.

Place 6 or 7 layers of phyllo pastry sheets in an 11×14×2-inch pan, brushing each sheet well with melted butter. Add spinach mixture, then place 7 or 8 layers of phyllo pastry sheets on filling, again buttering each sheet. Bake in a moderate 350-degree oven for about 30 minutes or until crust is a golden brown. Cut into squares before serving. Squares should be cut small and may be speared with a toothpick to keep phyllo pastry and filling together. *Yield: 16 squares*

Note: This method of making the recipe in a pan may be adapted to any of the phyllo pastry recipes given in this section.

MEAT ROLLS   *Bourekakia me Kreas*

4 tablespoons butter	¾ teaspoon pepper
1 pound ground beef (preferably round)	½ teaspoon curry powder
2 small onions, finely chopped	½ teaspoon cinnamon
2 cloves garlic, finely chopped	½ teaspoon allspice
1 cup water	1 8-ounce can tomato sauce
1 teaspoon salt	½ pound phyllo pastry sheets
	Melted butter

Melt the 4 tablespoons of butter in a heavy frying pan. Add meat, onions, and garlic, and brown well, stirring constantly, until onion is slightly cooked and meat is well browned. Add ¼ cup of the water so that the meat will not stick to the pan. Add the spices and adjust seasonings if desired. Add the tomato sauce and remaining water and stir until mixture begins to boil. Cover pan and simmer about ½ hour or until meat is thoroughly cooked. Stir occasionally. Allow to cool slightly, then drain meat mixture to eliminate excess liquid.

Take a portion of a sheet of phyllo pastry, about 6 inches long and 4 inches wide, and brush with melted butter. Place 1 teaspoon of the mixture at end of pastry, fold up once, and then turn in sides and roll. Brush with butter on all sides and place on a cooky sheet. Bake in a hot 450-degree oven for about 15 minutes until lightly browned. Allow to cool slightly. Serve warm. *Yield: 100 pieces*

SOUPS and SAUCES

SOUPS AND SAUCES

Soups and sauces play an important, if not the most important, part in Greek cooking, and are closely affiliated with the traditions of Greek holy days and festivals.

Lentil soup, a favorite from the time of the ancient Greeks, is still served on Holy Friday during the Lenten period, and bean soup is the mainstay of the Greek villager, who eats it every Friday with toursi* and sliced raw onion.

Two of the three major sauces in Greek cooking are a simple tomato sauce used in many meat and chicken dishes, and the pungent garlic sauce, *skordalia*, thickened with mashed potatoes, walnuts, or bread and served with fish, beets, cucumbers, and eggplant.

The most famous sauce is *avgolemono*, a tart, creamy sauce of eggs and lemon juice, which runs like a golden thread through Greek cooking. It is added to soups and stews and is served with many meat and vegetable dishes. It is an essential ingredient in the traditional Easter soup, known as mageritsa.* At midnight of Easter morn, the Greek places his lighted Resurrection candle on his table and breaks the Lenten fast with *mageritsa*, bread, cheese, and eggs.

SOUPS

CHICKEN SOUP WITH AVGOLEMONO SAUCE (Egg and Lemon Sauce) *Soupa Avgolemono*

Chicken Soup:

1 4–5-pound stewing hen, ready to cook	1 onion
	1 stalk celery
A few peppercorns	Salt
1 small carrot	1 cup rice, fide,* or kritharaki*

Wash hen and place in heavy kettle. Cover with boiling water and add peppercorns, carrot, onion, and celery stalk. Cover and simmer over low heat for 2 to 4 hours, or until hen is tender, adding salt to taste during last hour of cooking. Strain broth and remove extra fat. Add rice, *fide*, or *kritharaki* and continue to cook until rice or pasta is tender. Remove broth from heat and wait for boiling to stop. Add either of the *avgolemono* sauces below according to directions. *8–10 servings*

Avgolemono Sauce for Soup–Method I:

> 4 eggs
> 2 lemons, juice of

Beat eggs well and gradually beat in lemon juice. Add hot broth slowly to egg sauce, beating constantly. Return soup to heat and stir vigorously until thickened.

Avgolemono Sauce for Soup–Method II:

> 4 eggs, separated
> 2 lemons, juice of

Beat egg whites until they form soft points. Add yolks one at a time and continue beating. Gradually beat in lemon juice. Add broth slowly to egg sauce, return soup to heat, and stir furiously until thickened.

MAGERITSA (Easter Soup)

> 1 lamb tripe
> 1 baby lamb intestine
>   (optional)
> 1 baby lamb lung
> 1 lamb heart
> 1 lamb liver
> 2 lemons, juice of
>
> 3 bunches scallions, finely
>   chopped
> ¼ pound butter
> ½ cup chopped dill
> Salt and pepper
> ⅓–½ cup raw rice
> AVGOLEMONO SAUCE

Wash entrails and internal meats. If intestines are used, turn inside out and wash thoroughly. Scald tripe and cover with fresh, salted water. Bring to a boil and simmer for 40 minutes. Soak remaining meats for 30 minutes in cold water with the lemon juice. Drain and add to tripe for last 10 minutes of cooking. Strain, reserving broth, and cool. Put meat through a meat grinder, using the coarse blade.

Sauté scallions in butter until soft and add to meat along with the dill and salt and pepper to taste. Add broth and more water if necessary to cover, bring to a boil, and simmer, covered, for at least 3 hours. Add rice about 20 minutes before soup is ready to be served. Add either of the *avgolemono* sauces according to directions. *6–8 servings*

VARIATION: Add 1 to 2 tablespoons tomato paste diluted in broth.

GIOUVARLAKIA (Meatball Soup)

1 pound ground meat, lamb, or beef	*Salt and pepper*
1 small onion, grated	*Parsley, finely chopped*
¼ cup raw rice	*Meat stock*
Mint, chopped, to taste	*1 egg (optional)*

Combine meat, onion, rice, mint, and salt and pepper to taste and form tiny, marble-size meatballs. Roll in chopped parsley and drop into simmering stock. Cook until meat is tender, approximately 35 minutes. If desired, the ground meat may be moistened with 1 egg beaten with a little water. *4–6 servings*

VARIATIONS:

I. Omit parsley. Roll meatballs in flour and drop into simmering stock. When meat is tender, add AVGOLEMONO SAUCE according to directions.

II. If no stock is available, use bouillon cubes dissolved in water, or melt ¼ cup butter and add 2 tablespoons flour and salt and pepper to taste. Add 3 cups water to make a thin sauce and cook, stirring, until smooth. Bring sauce to a boil, add meatballs, and cook until meat is tender.

LAMB BROTH WITH VEGETABLES   *Arni Zoumo*

3 pounds lamb—shoulder,
   breast, neck, or shank—cut
   into pieces
3 quarts water
Butter or olive oil (optional)
3 stalks celery
3 carrots
3 onions
½ cup fide* or kritharaki*
Salt and pepper
AVGOLEMONO SAUCE

Bring lamb and water slowly to a boil. Chop vegetables and, if desired, sauté 5 to 10 minutes in butter or olive oil before adding to broth. Cover and simmer over low heat for 3 to 4 hours until tender. Add *fide* or *kritharaki* and salt and pepper to taste and cook for 20 minutes longer or until pasta is cooked. Add *avgolemono* sauce according to directions. *8–10 servings*

BEEF SOUP WITH PASTA   *Soupa Vothini me Rizi*

Beef bones or beef shank
2 onions, chopped
1 cup chopped celery and
   leaves
3 tablespoons butter
1 2½ can tomatoes
¾ cup rice, orzo,* or egg
   noodles
Salt and pepper to taste

Cover beef bones with water and bring to a boil. Add can tomatoes. Sauté chopped vegetables in butter for 10 minutes. Add to bones and bring to a boil. Simmer for 2 hours, or until meat is tender. Strain and press vegetables through a sieve. Add rice, *orzo*, or noodles and cook until tender. If beef shank is used, remove meat from bones when tender, cut in small pieces, and add to soup. *6–8 servings*

TRIPE SOUP   *Patsa*

2 pounds honeycomb tripe
8 pigs' feet
Salt and freshly ground black
   pepper
4–6 cloves garlic
3 eggs
4 tablespoons tarragon vinegar
Paprika and hot red pepper

Wash tripe in several changes of cold water. Drain. Cover tripe and pigs' feet with cold water and bring to a boil. Add salt, pepper, and 2 to 4 cloves garlic, not chopped. Simmer until meat is tender. Remove tripe and pigs' feet from broth, discard bones, and chop meat into small pieces. Set aside.

Strain broth. Beat eggs until light and slowly beat in the vinegar. Add 2 cloves garlic, minced, and gradually add the broth, beating constantly. Add meat and stir.

Patsa can be served hot or cold. If served hot, paprika and red pepper are added to taste. If served cold, it is allowed to jell and is then cut into diamond-shaped portions. Paprika and red pepper are added to taste. *6–8 servings*

FISH SOUP *Psarosoupa*

1 cup diced celery	Salt and pepper to taste
½ cup diced carrot	6 sprigs parsley, chopped
2 medium onions, diced	¼ pound fide*
1 or 2 leeks, chopped	2 pounds fish: sea bass, black
1 cup diced potatoes	fish, cod fillet, or any fatty
3 tablespoons olive oil	fish
2 quarts water or stock	Salt
1 cup white wine (optional)	Flour
1 ½ 2½ can tomatoes	

Sauté vegetables in olive oil for 5 to 10 minutes. Add water or stock, tomatoes, and seasonings. If desired, 1 cup white wine may be added in place of 1 cup water or stock. Simmer until vegetables are tender. Add *fide* and cook until *pasta* is tender. Meanwhile sprinkle fish with salt and roll in flour. Wrap in cheesecloth and tie ends loosely. When *pasta* is cooked, add fish and cook until tender. Remove fish and flake flesh, discarding skin and bone. Add flaked fish to soup. *8–10 servings*

VARIATION: Omit tomatoes. After fish is tender, remove, and add AVGOLEMONO SAUCE according to directions. ½ cup rice may be substituted for *fide*.

LENTIL SOUP *Faki*

1 pound lentils
2½ quarts water
2 medium onions, chopped
2 stalks celery, chopped
1 carrot, chopped (optional)
6 sprigs parsley, chopped
1 clove garlic, chopped
½ cup olive oil

1 tablespoon tomato paste
Bay leaf
Salt to taste
2 tablespoons vinegar, wine, or tarragon
1½ tablespoons flour (optional)
3 tablespoons wine vinegar (optional)

Soak lentils in water overnight. Next day, sauté vegetables and garlic in olive oil and add to lentils along with tomato paste, parsley, and bay leaf. Bring to a boil and simmer until lentils are tender. In last 15 minutes of cooking add salt. Stir in vinegar before serving. If desired, mix flour and wine vinegar to a paste and add to soup to thicken. *6–8 servings*

Note: ½ teaspoon oregano and ½ cup cooked tomatoes may be added just before soup is thickened.

BEAN SOUP *Fassoulada*

1 pound Yankee beans, lima beans, or chick-peas
½ cup olive oil
2 large onions, chopped
2 cloves garlic, minced
Pepper to taste

1 6-ounce can tomato purée or 1 pound can peeled tomatoes
3 quarts water
1 sprig mint (1 teaspoon dried mint)
Salt to taste

Soak beans overnight in water to cover. Next day add oil, onions, garlic, pepper, and tomato purée or tomatoes to the 3 quarts water and bring to a boil. Add drained beans. Simmer for about 2 hours or until beans are tender. In last 15 minutes of cooking add mint and salt. *6–8 servings*

BEANS PLAKI   *Fassoulia Plaki*

1 pound lima beans, black-eyed
   peas, or kidney beans
3 cloves garlic, minced
2 sprigs parsley, chopped
1 cup celery, chopped
4–5 medium onions, thickly
   sliced (optional)
1 cup carrots, chopped

½ cup olive oil
½ 6-ounce can tomato paste
2 quarts water
Salt and pepper
Bay leaf, crumbled
¼ teaspoon oregano
¼ teaspoon thyme

Soak beans overnight and cook until tender as directed on package. Drain. Sauté vegetables and garlic in olive oil; add tomato paste. Add the water, salt and pepper, parsley, bay leaf, oregano, and thyme, and simmer until vegetables are tender and most of the liquid has cooked away. Add beans, mix well, and cook 10 minutes longer. Allow to stand ½ hour before serving. *6–8 servings*

VARIATION: Use 3 quarts water and cook vegetables and pre-soaked beans together for about 1 hour or until done.

TOMATO SOUP   *Domatosoupa*

1 onion, chopped
1 green pepper, chopped (optional)
4 tablespoons olive oil
4 or 5 fresh tomatoes, peeled
   and diced

½ cup raw rice or orzo*
4–6 cups water
Salt and pepper to taste
½ cup parsley, chopped

Sauté onion and green pepper in olive oil until vegetables are soft. Add tomatoes and rice or *orzo* and continue to sauté for about 5 minutes longer. Add water, salt and pepper, and parsley. Bring to a boil and simmer for 20 minutes or until rice is tender. *4–6 servings*

POTATO SOUP   *Patatosoupa*

1 medium onion, finely chopped
4 tablespoons butter
2 tablespoons flour
1 quart hot broth
1 quart hot water

1½ pounds potatoes, peeled and
   diced
Salt to taste
2 egg yolks
1 cup milk

Sauté onion in 2 tablespoons of the butter until soft. Add flour and stir until bubbly. Add hot broth and water. Stir to blend. Add potatoes and salt. Bring to a rapid boil, cover, and boil for 30 minutes. Strain, pressing vegetables through sieve. Return soup to heat and bring back to a boil. When ready to serve, remove from heat and gradually stir in egg yolks beaten with the milk and a little of the hot soup. Stir in remaining butter and serve hot. *8–10 servings*

BARLEY SOUP   *Kritharosoupa*

½ cup barley	2 cups milk
1 quart broth	2 egg yolks
1 quart water	½ cup grated Parmesan cheese
Salt	3–4 tablespoons butter

Several hours prior to making soup, soak barley in water to cover. Put broth and the 1 quart water in a pot and bring to a boil. Drain and add barley and salt. Cover and simmer, stirring occasionally, until barley is almost cooked. Add milk and continue cooking until barley is soft. When ready to serve, remove from heat and gradually stir in egg yolks beaten with a little of the hot soup. Stir in cheese and butter. Serve hot. *8–10 servings*

BUTTERMILK SOUP   *Taratori*

3–5 walnuts, shelled	1 quart buttermilk or 1 quart
Dash of salt	yogurt diluted with ½ cup
1 clove garlic	cold water or 6 ice cubes
¼ cup olive oil	1 or more cucumbers, chopped
1 tablespoon water	Salt and pepper to taste
1 tablespoon vinegar	

In a mortar mash nuts with salt. Add garlic and oil and continue to mash to a paste. Mash in water and vinegar. Stir mixture into chilled buttermilk or diluted yogurt. Add chopped cucumber and season with salt and pepper. Serve cold. *4 servings*

HOMEMADE PASTA FOR SOUP

Trahana (sweet)–Basic Recipe:

Milk	Flour
Farina	Salt

Start with 1 to 2 quarts milk. Add to this equal quantities of farina and flour, mixed, to make a soft dough. Add to dough 1 teaspoon salt per quart milk used. Form dough into egg-size pieces, flatten out on the palms of the hands, and lay on clean tablecloth to dry. When dry on one side, turn over. When thoroughly dry, crumble each little round by hand and dry thoroughly again. Break into rice-size morsels and keep out in sun for 3 or 4 days to dry some more. Store in airtight cans. Use in soups as a fide* or in place of rice.

Trahana (sweet and sour):
Use same method as above but instead of all milk, start out with half milk and half yogurt.

Trahana (sour):
Use all yogurt or sour milk for the liquid.

Trahana with Tomato:
Boil several tomatoes, two or three onions, a green pepper, and a stalk or two of celery until very tender. Purée the vegetables and add the purée to evaporated milk. Use this mixture for liquid in basic recipe.

SAUCES

AVGOLEMONO SAUCE I *Saltsa Avgolemono*

2 or 3 eggs, separated	1 or 2 lemons, juice of
Dash of salt	1 cup boiling broth or stock

Beat egg whites with dash of salt until thick but not dry. Add yolks one at a time and beat until well blended. Gradually beat in lemon juice and the hot broth or stock. (Be sure to do this slowly and beat constantly so that eggs will not curdle.) Gradually stir into gravy or stew and cook, stirring rapidly, until sauce is thickened. Do not let mixture boil. *Yield: 1 cup*

AVGOLEMONO SAUCE II *Saltsa Avgolemono*

2 or 3 eggs	1 or 2 lemons, juice of
1 tablespoon cornstarch	1 cup boiling broth or stock

Beat the eggs. Beat in cornstarch and lemon juice. Slowly beat in hot stock. Gradually stir this sauce into liquid to be thickened and cook, stirring, until sauce coats the spoon. May be used on meatballs if desired. *Yield: 1 cup*

BARBECUE SAUCE I *Marinata*

2 cups red wine
3 or 4 lemons, juice of
1 medium onion, chopped
2 cloves garlic

1 teaspoon oregano
¼ cup chopped celery leaves
¼ cup shaved carrot

Combine all ingredients and pour over meat or poultry. Let stand overnight, turning meat or poultry occasionally. Use sauce to baste meat while broiling or barbecuing. *Yield: 2 cups*

BARBECUE SAUCE II *Marinata*

3 or 4 lemons, juice of
½ cup olive oil
2 cloves garlic, minced

1 teaspoon oregano
Salt and pepper to taste

Combine all ingredients and pour over meat or poultry. Let stand overnight and use the sauce to brush the meat or poultry while it is broiling or grilling. *Yield: 1 cup*

TOMATO SAUCE I *Saltsa Domatas*

6 tomatoes
2 tablespoons butter
1 small onion, finely chopped

1–2 cloves garlic, minced
2 tablespoons flour
Salt and pepper

Peel tomatoes and cut into thick slices. Place in heavy pan, without adding water, and simmer until very soft. Rub tomatoes through a sieve. Melt butter and in it cook onion and garlic until onion is golden and soft. Stir in flour and simmer until mixture is bubbly. Add the strained tomatoes and salt and pepper to taste, and continue cooking, stirring constantly, until sauce is thick. *Yield: about 2 cups*

This sauce may be used whenever tomato sauce is called for in lamb, chicken, or fish recipes. It may also be used over cooked macaroni.

VARIATION: Omit tomatoes and flour from above recipe. Add 1 6-ounce can tomato paste diluted with ½ can water to onion mixture, season to taste, and cook, stirring, until sauce is thick. *Yield: 1 cup*

TOMATO SAUCE II *Saltsa Domatas*

4 tablespoons minced onions	*1 teaspoon paprika*
1 cup tomato purée or sauce	*½ teaspoon pepper*
3 tablespoons wine vinegar	*½ teaspoon cinnamon*
1 teaspoon salt	*Dash of ground cloves*

Combine all ingredients in order listed and heat to boiling point. Serve with any meat, poultry, or fish that has been broiled, fried, or barbecued. *Yield: 1 cup*

FISH SAUCE *Saltsa Psariou*

1 clove garlic, chopped	*1 tablespoon parsley, chopped*
2 onions, minced	*½ cup water*
3 tablespoons olive oil	*½ cup dry white wine*
1 bay leaf	*1 lemon, juice of*
¼ teaspoon oregano	*Salt and pepper to taste*

Sauté garlic and onions in the olive oil until golden brown. Add bay leaf, oregano, and parsley and cook for a few minutes longer. Pour in the water, wine, and lemon juice. Season with salt and pepper and simmer over low heat for 20 minutes longer. Remove from heat and cool. Delicious served with fried fish. *Yield: 1 cup*

SAVORY SAUCE *Saltsa Savori*

1 head garlic, minced	*3 bay leaves*
2 cups olive oil	*Salt to taste*
1 cup wine vinegar	

Cook garlic in olive oil until lightly browned. Add vinegar and bay leaves. Simmer about 5 minutes. Pour over cold fried fish. *Yield: 2½–3 cups*

VINAIGRETTE SAUCE *Saltsa Ladoxeidou*

This sauce is the Greek oil-and-vinegar sauce to which pickled cucumbers, capers, parsley, and finely chopped hard-cooked eggs may be added.

In a bowl mix 1 or 2 spoonfuls of water with equal amounts of oil and vinegar (or according to taste). Season with salt and pepper and beat well. If desired, add some chopped pickled cucumbers, capers, parsley, and a finely chopped hard-cooked egg. Mix well.

This sauce must be mixed well each time before serving. Delicious over broiled or baked brains.

OLIVE OIL AND LEMON SAUCE   *Ladoxeido*

3 tablespoons olive oil
3 tablespoons lemon juice
1 teaspoon oregano

Beat olive oil and lemon juice until creamy. Beat in oregano. *Yield: ½ cup*

GARLIC SAUCE–THICK   *Skordalia*

6–7 cloves garlic
3 or 4 boiled potatoes, mashed
1 cup olive oil

⅔ cup vinegar
Salt and pepper to taste

Crush garlic in a ghoudi,* or mortar. Add mashed potatoes and pound well until blended to a paste. Add olive oil and vinegar alternately in very small amounts, stirring sauce briskly with the pestle. Add salt and pepper. Continue to stir in a rotary motion until sauce is stiff enough to hold its shape. *Yield: 2 cups*

GARLIC SAUCE–THIN   *Skordalia*

8 cloves garlic
Dash salt
4 large boiled potatoes, mashed

1 cup olive oil
2 lemons, juice of
1½ cups fish stock

Crush garlic with a dash of salt in a mortar or a heavy bowl. Add mashed potatoes and pound until well blended. Add olive oil and lemon juice alternately and keep pounding until ingredients are thoroughly blended. Add the stock slowly, stirring until sauce is at the creamy consistency desired. *Yield: 2½ cups*

GARLIC SAUCE WITH WALNUTS   *Skordalia me Karidia*

6 cloves garlic
½ teaspoon salt
1 pound whole walnuts, shelled
10 slices, or ½ loaf, dry bread

1 cup olive oil
½ cup vinegar
1 cup warm water
Salt to taste

Pound garlic in mortar with salt until well crushed. Add walnuts and pound to blend well. Thoroughly soak bread in water and squeeze to remove excess moisture. Add to garlic and pound until well mashed. Add olive oil and vinegar alternately, beating thoroughly after each addition. Add warm water; blend well. If a thinner sauce is preferred, add a little more warm water. Correct seasoning with salt to taste. *Yield: 3 cups*

GARLIC SAUCE WITH PIGNOLIA NUTS   *Skordalia*

6 cloves garlic	*½ cup vinegar or lemon juice*
1 teaspoon salt	*2½ cups olive oil*
½ cup pignolia nuts	*1 egg*
4 or 5 cups mashed potatoes or	
10 slices bread	

Mash garlic in mortar with salt. Add pignolia nuts and pound until well blended. Add potatoes, or bread that has been soaked in water to soften and squeezed to remove excess moisture. If a stronger garlic taste is desired, use only 3 or 4 cups potatoes. Transfer mixture to mixing bowl. Clean mortar with vinegar or lemon juice and add to sauce. Gradually add olive oil, beating with an electric beater until all oil is absorbed. Add the egg and continue beating until smooth. Add ½ cup warm water for a thinner sauce. Serve with fried or broiled fish, fried eggplant, squash, or boiled beets. *Yield: 4–5 cups*

CREAM SAUCE   *Béchamel* Sauce

½ cup butter
6 tablespoons flour
1 quart hot milk

1 teaspoon salt
Dash of white pepper

Melt butter in a saucepan, add flour, and stir until smooth. Remove from heat and gradually stir in milk. Use a wooden spoon while stirring to prevent sauce from sticking to bottom of saucepan. Return to heat and cook, stirring constantly, until sauce is smooth and thickened. Reduce heat and cook a few minutes longer. Stir in salt and pepper, cover tightly, and place over hot water to keep warm. *Yield: 4 cups*

MINT SAUCE   *Saltsa Diosmou*

1 cup mint leaves, chopped
1 tablespoon sugar
2 tablespoons vinegar

½ teaspoon salt
1 cup warm water

Put all ingredients in a bowl and stir to blend thoroughly. Serve in a sauceboat. This sauce is very good with cold meats. *Yield: 1½ cups*

HOLLANDAISE SAUCE

2 tablespoons vinegar
Salt and pepper to taste
2 egg yolks

1 cup butter, melted
1 teaspoon lemon juice
2 tablespoons water or milk

In top of double saucepan combine vinegar and salt and pepper. Bring to a boil over direct heat and simmer for a few minutes. Cool. Add egg yolks and half of butter. Place pan over hot water and mix sauce with a wire whisk until it becomes as thick as mayonnaise. Remove from heat and add remaining butter, a little at a time, stirring constantly. Add lemon juice and water or milk. Keep warm over hot but not simmering water until time to serve. *Yield: 1 cup*

MAYONNAISE   *Mayoneza*

5 egg yolks	*1 cup olive oil*
3–4 tablespoons prepared	*½ cup lemon juice*
mustard	

Beat egg yolks and mustard at medium speed in electric mixer until thick. Very slowly pour in olive oil alternately with lemon juice and continue beating until thick. *Yield: 2½ cups*

FISH

FISH AND SHELLFISH

Many fishing villages dot the 2500-mile coastline of Greece, but fishing is by no means confined to the gulfs and bays of the mainland. It is an active industry on the many islands surrounding Greece. Cyclades, Corfu, Chios, Lesbos, Samos, Crete, and the Dodecanese all have their share of fishing ports where the fishing boats anchor at dusk each evening to unload their catch.

Fish is plentiful in Grecian waters and is a favorite dish on Greek tables. It is broiled with oil and lemon, fried, braised in a savory tomato sauce, or baked. PSARI PLAKI, a baked fish, is traditionally served on Palm Sunday as part of the Lenten fast, and the entire forty days of Lent are no more strictly observed in any other country in the world than they are in Greece. There are no lapses of meat eating, party giving, or diversions of any kind throughout the entire Lenten season.

In general, the Greeks prefer cooking fish at high heat in hot oil to the more gentle cooking methods of poaching or sautéeing. They frequently marinate the fish in oil and lemon juice before frying it in olive oil.

In addition to barbouni,* palamida,* bakaliaros,* tsipoura,* and skoumbri,* the waters surrounding Greece yield many bivalves and shellfish. Oysters are plentiful, but are not considered a delicacy by the Greeks, who much prefer mussels, shrimp, and sea urchins.

After centuries of preparing fish, the Greeks have developed many interesting fish dishes to contribute to the world's cuisine.

PELOPONNESIAN FISH . FILLET *Peloponesiotiko Psari*

2 pounds frozen haddock or flounder	Salt to taste
	1 cup flour
2 lemons, juice of	1 cup salad oil
Monosodium glutamate	1–2 teaspoons oregano

While still frozen, cut each pound of fish into 6 pieces. Place in bowl and add lemon juice, monosodium glutamate, and salt. Allow to marinate for several hours. Put flour in small paper bag. Heat oil in skillet. Put each piece of fish in flour bag and shake until well coated. Fry in hot oil until golden brown on both sides, being careful not to overcook. (Overcooking causes the fish to become too dry.) Place cooked fish in bowl. Drain off all but ¼ cup oil in skillet, leaving bits of browned flour on bottom. Add oregano. Add the liquid in which the fish was marinated and cook, stirring in all brown bits from bottom and sides of skillet, until sauce is thickened. If necessary, add a little water and more salt to taste. Pour sauce over fish and cover bowl. Serve 15 minutes later. *6–8 servings*

MUSSELS WITH RICE *Midia Pilafi*

2–3 dozen mussels	*½ cup water*
Bunch of scallions or 2 onions,	*2½ cups boiling water*
* chopped*	*Salt to taste*
1 cup olive oil	*1 cup raw rice*
1 teaspoon tomato paste	

Prepare mussels by covering with cold water and soaking for ½ hour. Scrape with dull knife, removing rough parts of shell, and pull out hairy tuft if any shows. Rinse well. Sauté scallions or onions in oil. Add tomato paste, the ½ cup water, and mussels, cover, and steam until mussels open. Discard any that do not open. Add boiling water, salt, and rice. Do not shell mussels. Cover and cook until rice is tender. *4–6 servings*

VARIATION: Add ½ cup of currants along with rice.

BRAISED SHRIMP *Garides Yahni*

2 pounds shrimp	*2 cups canned Italian tomatoes*
5 onions, sliced	*1 teaspoon parsley, chopped*
½ cup olive oil	

Cook shrimp with shells in water to cover for 10 minutes or until tender. Drain, reserving 1 cup of the broth. Shell and de-vein shrimp. Sauté onions in olive oil. Add tomatoes, chopped parsley, and 1 cup shrimp broth and simmer for 20 minutes. Add shrimp. *4–6 servings*

VARIATION: Increase broth to 2 cups and bring to a boil. Add salt to taste. Add 1 cup rice, cover, and cook until rice is tender. Add shrimp.

ISLAND SHRIMP   *Garides Nisiotikes*

3 tablespoons butter
3 tablespoons flour
2 cups milk
½ teaspoon prepared horse-radish

Garlic powder to taste
2 tablespoons ketchup
1 pound shrimp, cleaned and cooked
Cooked rice

Blend butter and flour over low heat. Gradually stir in milk and cook, stirring, until sauce is smooth and thickened. Stir in horse-radish, garlic powder, and ketchup. Add shrimp. Serve over cooked rice. If desired, rice may be cooked in broth in which shrimp were poached. *4 servings*

VARIATION: Tuna, salmon, or lobster may be substituted for shrimp.

BROILED SHRIMP   *Garides tis Skaras*

1 pound shrimp
Olive oil

Sauce:
1 lemon, juice of
⅓ cup olive oil
1 tablespoon dill, finely chopped

Wash and clean shrimp. Brush with olive oil and broil about 3 inches from heat for 5 minutes. Serve with sauce made by combining lemon juice, olive oil, and dill. *3–4 servings*

FRIED SHRIMP   *Garides Tighanites*

1 pound shrimp
4 tablespoons butter

Sauce:
1 lemon, juice of
⅓ cup olive oil
1 tablespoon parsley or dill,
finely chopped

Wash and clean shrimp. Melt butter in skillet and in it sauté shrimp for 10 minutes, turning occasionally with wooden spoon, until lightly browned on both sides. Serve with sauce made by combining lemon juice, olive oil, and parsley or dill. *3–4 servings*

FISH PLAKI   *Psari Plaki*

Use 3 pounds baking fish—striped bass, sea bass, or bluefish, or 2 pounds halibut, cod, or haddock fillets.

Salt and pepper
Oregano
½ cup olive oil
3 fresh tomatoes, sliced
3 scallions, chopped
1 cup parsley, chopped
1 clove garlic, finely minced

20 salted butter crackers, finely
* ground*
Butter
2 large onions, sliced into rings
Lemon slices
1 cup water

Place fish in greased baking pan and sprinkle with salt and pepper, oregano, and olive oil. Add tomato slices, scallions, parsley, and garlic. Top with cracker crumbs, dot with butter, and decorate with onion rings and lemon slices. Add water. Bake at 350 degrees for 45 minutes. *6 servings*

VARIATION: The tomatoes, scallions, parsley, and garlic may be sautéed in oil before they are added to baking dish.

FISH WITH MAYONNAISE SAUCE   *Psari Mayoneza*

Note: This recipe should be prepared a day before it is served, and tastes best with homemade mayonnaise.

1 striped bass, cleaned, 5
  pounds
Salt
2 carrots, sliced

2 celery stalks, sliced
4 scallions, chopped
Water to cover

Wash and scale fish. Salt well. Tie in cheesecloth and place on rack in fish kettle with carrots, celery, and scallions. Add water and bring to a simmer. Cover kettle and simmer fish for 35 minutes. Cool in broth. Remove fish and place on platter. Remove cheesecloth.

Mayonnaise:

5 egg yolks
3–4 tablespoons prepared
  mustard

1 cup olive oil
½ cup lemon juice

Beat egg yolks and mustard in an electric mixer at medium speed until thick. (If milder sauce is preferred, use half the amount of mustard specified.) Very slowly pour in olive oil and lemon juice and continue to beat until sauce is smooth and thick. Pour over fish.

Garnish with lemon slices. *8 servings*

CODFISH STEW   *Bakaliaro Yahni*

1 box boneless salt cod or 1
  large dried codfish with bones
2 pounds small white onions
½ 6-ounce can tomato paste
¾ cup water

1 bay leaf
Garlic to taste
Salt and pepper to taste
½ cup olive oil
Small potatoes (optional)

Soak codfish in cold water overnight, changing water a few times. Put all ingredients except potatoes in a stewing kettle, cover, and bring to a boil. Add potatoes. Cook over low heat for about 1 hour. If liquid cooks away, add a little more water as needed. *6 servings*

FISH WITH WALNUT SAUCE *Psari me Skordalia*

⅓ cup olive oil	Salt and pepper to taste
1 tablespoon flour	Meats from 1 pound walnuts in
1 teaspoon paprika	shells, chopped and mashed
1 quart warm water	½–1 teaspoon garlic powder or
1 sea bass (approximately 3	1 clove garlic, mashed
pounds)	Parsley, chopped

Heat oil; add flour and cook, stirring, until brown. Add paprika. Slowly stir in the warm water. Add fish and salt and pepper and simmer for 30 to 40 minutes. Allow fish to cool in broth. To walnut meats add garlic powder or clove garlic. Work in a little of the broth to make a smooth paste. Gradually stir in rest of the broth. Carefully place whole fish on platter. Pour walnut sauce over fish to cover and decorate with parsley. Serve cold. *6 servings*

SQUID *Kalamaria Yemista*

1 pound kalamaria*	1 bay leaf, crumbled
2–3 onions, chopped	½ cup raw rice
2–3 cloves garlic, chopped	Currants (optional)
½ cup oil	Parsley or dill, chopped
Salt and pepper to taste	1½ cups boiling water
1 cup tomato sauce	

Use small, tender *kalamaria*.

To prepare *kalamaria*, discard celluloid backbone, ink sac, and head. Chop tentacles and set aside. Wash squid thoroughly and soak in water until ready to use. Brown onions and garlic in oil. Add salt and pepper, tomato sauce, and bay leaf. Add rice, currants, parsley or dill, and the chopped tentacles. Stuff squid with this mixture. Place in oiled casserole and pour any remaining stuffing mixture on top. Add the water and correct seasoning. Cover and simmer for 25 minutes. *4–6 servings*

OCTOPUS IN RED WINE SAUCE *Oktapodi Krassato*

2 pounds fresh octopus, well
   pounded
2 medium onions, finely
   chopped

½ cup olive oil
Salt and pepper
1 bay leaf
1 cup red wine

Make sure the octopus has been well beaten to tenderize it when you buy it. Wash it carefully and discard the ink sac. Cut octopus into bite-size pieces. Sauté the onions in the olive oil until soft and golden. Add octopus, salt and pepper, and bay leaf and stew for 10 minutes. Add wine and enough water to cover. Bring to a boil, cover, and simmer for about 1 hour or until octopus is tender.

Octopus is served as a hot hors d'oeuvre, or may be served as a main dish with RICE PILAF. *4 servings*

OCTOPUS WITH ONIONS AND TOMATO *Oktapodi Yahni*

2 pounds fresh octopus, well
   pounded
4 large onions, finely chopped

1 cup olive oil
2 tablespoons tomato paste
Salt and pepper

Be sure the octopus has been well pounded to tenderize it. Clean it thoroughly and discard the ink sac. Cut octopus into bite-size pieces. Sauté onions in olive oil until soft and golden. Add octopus, tomato paste, and salt and pepper and stew for 10 minutes. Add enough water to cover. Bring to a boil, cover, and simmer for about 1 hour or until octopus is tender.

Serve as a hot hors d'oeuvre or as a main dish with RICE PILAF. *4 servings*

STUFFED FISH *Psari Yemisto*

A 5-pound striped bass
Salt
2–3 onions, chopped
3 stalks celery, chopped
¼ cup olive oil
3 hard-cooked eggs, chopped

½ pound cooked shrimp,
   chopped
½ cup bread crumbs
About 1 cup fish or shrimp stock
¼ cup butter
Lemon slices

Clean, wash, and salt fish. Sauté onion and celery in olive oil until tender. Add chopped eggs and shrimp. Add bread crumbs and enough stock to moisten; stuffing should not be runny. Stuff fish and skewer or sew opening closed. Place in oiled baking pan and dot with butter. Bake in a moderate 350-degree oven for about 1 hour or until flesh flakes easily, basting occasionally with butter and juices in pan. Garnish with lemon slices and serve hot or cold. *8 servings*

BROILED FISH *Psari tis Skaras*

Porgies, striped bass, smelts, or
  flounder
Salt

Oregano
Lemon juice
Olive oil

Clean, wash, and salt fish and sprinkle with oregano. Broil a few inches from heat, basting with lemon juice mixed with olive oil.

BAKED HALIBUT OR COD STEAKS *Psari Psito*

½ cup mayonnaise
1½ lemons, juice of
Salt and pepper to taste

Parsley, chopped
2 pounds fish steaks

Combine mayonnaise, lemon juice, salt and pepper, and parsley. Mix well and spread on steaks. Bake in a 350-degree oven for 20 minutes. Brown under broiler. *6 servings*

FRIED FISH *Psari Tighanito*

Mackerel, porgies, fillets, or fish
  roe
Salt

Flour or cracker meal
Oil

Clean, wash, and salt fish. Dip in flour or cracker meal. Fry in about 1 inch hot oil in skillet until well browned on both sides.

BROILED MACKEREL WITH POLITIKO SAUCE   *Skoumbri tis Skaras me Saltsa Politiki*

Broil mackerel, basting with lemon juice. When cooked, place on platter and top with the following sauce:

½–¾ cup olive oil   *1 onion, thinly sliced*
2 lemons, juice of   *1 cup parsley, chopped*
2 tablespoons ice water

Beat olive oil and lemon juice until thick and creamy. Beat in ice water. Stir in onion and parsley and serve immediately.

VARIATION: Add a little oregano in place of, or along with, the parsley.

COD KAPAMA   *Bakaliaro Kapama*

Salt   *Salt and pepper*
Flour   *¼ teaspoon cinnamon*
1 pound fresh cod   *⅓ cup raisins or currants*
2 large onions, finely sliced *1 cup water or more*
½ cup olive oil

Wash, salt, and flour fish. In a large skillet sauté onions in oil, add seasonings, raisins or currants, and water, and bring to a boil. Add fish and simmer for 15 to 20 minutes or until cooked. *4 servings*

VARIATION: Add 3 to 4 potatoes, sliced, before adding fish. Simmer sauce and potatoes for 10 minutes, add fish, and continue to cook until fish and potatoes are tender.

FISH WITH SAVORY SAUCE   *Psari Savori*

Flour   *2 cloves garlic, chopped*
Salt   *¼ cup wine vinegar*
Porgies, bluefish, or halibut   *1 6-ounce can tomato paste*
Olive oil   *1 can water or more*
2 bay leaves   *Salt and pepper to taste*

Flour and salt fish. Fry fish in 1 inch hot oil in skillet until browned. Arrange cooked fish in casserole. Pour off all but about ½ cup of the olive oil in skillet. Remove skillet from heat. Add bay leaves and garlic and stir in vinegar, tomato paste, water, and salt and pepper. Return to heat and simmer for 15 to 20 minutes. Pour over cooked fish. Cover immediately and allow to stand at least 1 hour before serving. Serve warm or cold.

FRIED COD *Bakaliaro Tighanito*

1 salted cod	1 teaspoon baking powder
1½ cups flour	Water
½ teaspoon salt	Oil for frying
Dash of pepper	GARLIC SAUCE (Skordalia)

Soak cod overnight in water to cover. Drain and cut into 8 to 10 pieces. Combine flour, salt, pepper, and baking powder with enough water to make a batter the consistency of a thin white sauce. Dip pieces of cod in batter and fry in 1 inch hot oil in skillet until golden brown. Drain on absorbent paper and serve with garlic sauce. *4–5 servings*

FRIED BABY SQUID *Kalamaria Tighanita*

Use deep frying pan with at least 1 inch of oil. Wash and clean squid. Cut larger squid into small pieces. Fry for about 15 minutes until well browned.

Baby squid, cut in small pieces, may be served as appetizers when fried in butter.

Serve with LEMON AND OIL SAUCE or SKORDALIA.

POULTRY

POULTRY

Chicken, although not too plentiful, is a favorite dish in Greece. It is sautéed, broiled, and stewed with many vegetables in savory sauces. However to a Greek there is only one way to roast a bird and that is stuffed with a robust mixture of chopped vegetables, nuts, fruit, chopped meat, and rice, seasoned with several herbs and aromatic spices. It will be a new taste experience for anyone who has never enjoyed a roast chicken or turkey *à la grecque*.

In the cooking of fowl in Greece, lemon plays an important role. The cut-up bird is frequently marinated in olive oil and lemon juice and flavored with oregano before it is broiled or pot-roasted, and never is a bird oven-roasted without having its skin liberally anointed with lemon juice both before and during cooking.

Again the famous Greek avgolemono sauce* is poured over cooked chicken and, when the chicken is flavored with scallions and chopped dill, it is a dish never to be forgotten.

CHICKEN FRICASEE WITH PARSLEY SAUCE *Kota Frikase me Maïtano*

4-pound chicken cut into serving pieces	1½ teaspoons salt
4 tablespoons oil	Dash of pepper
1 clove garlic, sliced	1½ cups water

Wash chicken. Heat oil and brown garlic in it. Remove garlic and cook chicken in the oil until brown on all sides. Season with salt and pepper. Add water and cook, covered, until tender. Serve with parsley sauce.

Parsley Sauce:

2 tablespoons butter	½ cup parsley, chopped
2 tablespoons flour	½ teaspoon salt
1 cup light cream or top milk	Yolks of 2 eggs
1 cup chicken stock	1 teaspoon lemon juice

Melt butter and add flour. Blend well and add cream and stock slowly, stirring constantly, until sauce is smooth and thickened. Add parsley and salt and bring sauce to a boil. Beat egg yolks and lemon juice with a little of the hot sauce and gradually stir into remaining sauce. Cook, stirring, over low heat for about 3 minutes or until eggs are cooked. Pour over chicken on serving platter. *6 servings*

CHICKEN PILAF *Kotopoulo Atzem Pilafi*

3-pound chicken cut into serving
    pieces
8 tablespoons butter
Salt and pepper to taste
Dash cinnamon, clove, and all-
    spice

3 medium onions, chopped
1 6-ounce can tomato paste
¾ cup cold water
2 cups boiling water
1 cup raw rice

Brown chicken in 4 tablespoons of the butter with salt and pepper and spices. Add onions and brown. Add tomato paste and the cold water. Cover and simmer until chicken is tender. Add boiling water. Stir in rice, cover, and simmer for 20 minutes. When ready to serve, heat remaining butter until it turns brown and pour over chicken and rice. *4 servings*

BAKED CHICKEN PILAF *Kotopoulo Pilafi tou Fournou*

2½–3-pound chicken cut into
    serving pieces
1 clove garlic or garlic salt to
    taste
1 tablespoon tomato paste

Salt and pepper
⅓ cup butter
2½ cups boiling water
1 teaspoon salt
1 cup raw rice

Rub chicken pieces with garlic or sprinkle with garlic salt. Put pieces in an oiled baking dish or casserole and coat with tomato paste. Sprinkle with salt and pepper and dot with butter. Add ½ cup of the water and bake in a 350-degree oven for 30 minutes, turning chicken pieces once. Add remaining water, the 1 teaspoon salt, and the rice. Stir carefully to make sure that all the rice sinks to the bottom of the casserole and the chicken pieces are on the top. Increase oven heat to 400 degrees and continue baking for 30 minutes or until rice is tender. *4 servings*

BROILED CHICKEN OREGANO　*Kotopoulo Riganato tis Skaras*

2½–3-pound broiler or fryer cut into serving pieces
1 clove garlic, cut
Salt and pepper

Oregano
1½ lemons, juice of
⅓ cup butter, melted

Several hours before serving, or the day before, rub chicken pieces with garlic and place in a deep china or earthenware bowl. Sprinkle with salt and pepper, oregano, and lemon juice. Cover bowl and refrigerate.

When ready to cook, arrange chicken pieces on broiler rack and baste with melted butter. Add remaining marinade to butter and broil 3 to 4 inches from heat for 15 to 20 minutes on each side, basting often. *4 servings*

This chicken is delicious broiled over charcoal.

CHICKEN AND OKRA　*Kotopoulo me Bamyes*

1 pound fresh okra or 2 boxes frozen okra
1 lemon, juice of
4 tablespoons butter

3–4-pound chicken cut into serving pieces
1 onion, chopped
1 cup water
1 1-pound can plum tomatoes

For fresh okra wash and cut off stems, place in dish, and sprinkle with lemon juice. If using frozen okra just remove from boxes and sprinkle with lemon juice. In Dutch oven melt butter and in it brown chicken and onion until golden. Add water, tomatoes, and okra, including juice. Cover and cook for 1 hour over low heat. *4–6 servings*

VARIATION: Substitute green peas or artichokes for the okra.

CHICKEN WITH SCALLIONS　*Kotopoulo me Kremidakia Freska*

3–4-pound chicken cut into serving pieces
5 tablespoons butter
Salt and pepper to taste
1 cup hot water

6 bunches scallions, cleaned and cut into 1-inch pieces
3 eggs
1 lemon, juice of

Wash chicken pieces. In Dutch oven melt butter and in it brown chicken until golden on all sides. Sprinkle with salt and pepper and add hot water and scallions. Cover and cook over low heat for 1 hour. Beat eggs, adding lemon juice slowly. Add some broth from pan, beating eggs constantly to prevent curdling. Then add egg mixture to pan, stirring for a minute or so to keep it from curdling. The heat under pan must be lowered when egg mixture is being added to the sauce and the sauce must not be allowed to boil after eggs are added. *4–6 servings*

POT-ROAST CHICKEN *Kotopoulo Kapakoti*

1 chicken (fryer)
Salt and pepper to taste
¼ cup olive oil

1 lemon, juice of
Oregano to taste

Marinate chicken with salt and pepper in 2 tablespoons of the olive oil, the lemon juice, and oregano. Turn occasionally. Heat Dutch oven. Add rest of oil and brown chicken. Add marinade and a little water, cover, and simmer over low heat for about 1 hour or until chicken is tender. *4 servings*

CHICKEN KAPAMA *Kota Kapama*

1 chicken or capon cut into
*   serving pieces*
Salt and pepper
Dash cinnamon
6 tablespoons butter
2 cups canned tomatoes
1 6-ounce can tomato paste

1 teaspoon sugar
¾ cup water
3 sticks cinnamon
3 onions, minced
3 cloves garlic, minced
1 pound macaroni
Grated cheese

Sprinkle chicken with salt and pepper and cinnamon. In heavy kettle melt 2 tablespoons of the butter and in it brown chicken until golden on all sides. Combine tomatoes, tomato paste, sugar, and water and pour sauce over chicken. Add cinnamon sticks. Sauté minced onion and garlic in another 2 tablespoons butter and add to chicken. Bring sauce to a boil, cover, and simmer until chicken is tender.

Cook macaroni according to directions on package. Drain and empty into serving dish. Brown remaining butter and pour over macaroni. Pour over sauce from chicken and sprinkle with grated cheese. Serve chicken separately. *6 servings*

CHICKEN WITH DILL SAUCE *Kota me Anitho*

1 roasting chicken cut into serving pieces
4 tablespoons butter
1½ cups boiling water

Salt to taste
3 bunches scallions, sliced
Fresh dill or parsley, chopped

Brown chicken on all sides in half the butter. Add boiling water and salt. Sauté sliced scallions and dill in remaining butter. Add to chicken. Cover and simmer until chicken is tender.

Add AVGOLEMONO SAUCE as follows:

2–3 eggs
1½ lemons, juice of

Separate eggs. Beat egg whites until stiff, add yolks and lemon juice, and continue beating. Gradually beat in the hot liquid from the chicken. Pour over chicken and serve immediately. *4–6 servings*

CHICKEN WITH BARBECUE SAUCE *Kotopoulo Marinato*

½ cup butter, melted
1½ teaspoons salt
1 large clove garlic, minced
2 tablespoons Worcestershire
   sauce

½ cup ketchup
1 small onion, diced
1 chicken, fryer or broiler, cut
   into serving pieces

Melt butter and combine with salt, garlic, Worcestershire sauce, ketchup, and onion. Brush on chicken and marinate for several hours. Bake in a 350-degree oven for 45 minutes. Place under broiler for 5 minutes to crisp and brown chicken, and serve. *4 servings*

CHICKEN AND SAUERKRAUT *Kotopoulo me Lahano Toursi*

1 chicken, fryer or broiler, cut
   into serving pieces
4 tablespoons butter
Salt and pepper
2 onions, chopped

1 cup celery, chopped
1 1-pound can tomatoes
1 pound sauerkraut
½ lemon, sliced
2 cinnamon sticks

Brown chicken in butter in a heavy kettle until golden on all sides. Sprinkle with salt and pepper. Add onions, celery, and, after a few more minutes of browning, add tomatoes. Rinse sauerkraut and add to kettle with slices of lemon and cinnamon sticks. Simmer over low heat for 1 to 1½ hours. *4–6 servings*

CHICKEN STEFADO   *Kotopoulo Stefado*

*1 chicken (3–4 pounds) cut
    into serving pieces
4 tablespoons oil or butter
2–3 onions, grated
1 6-ounce can tomato paste
Water*

*Mixed spices
Bay leaves
Whole white onions
Kefalotiri* or Romano cheese,
    cubed*

Brown chicken in oil or butter. Add onions and tomato paste with
enough water to cover. Add mixed spices and bay leaves tied in a
cloth bag. Remove chicken when cooked. Add whole white onions
and hard cheese to sauce remaining in kettle and cook until tender.
Cheese may be fried in oil first before being added to sauce. Add
chicken, heat, and serve. *4–6 servings*

CHICKEN STEW   *Kota Yahni*

*1 chicken cut into serving pieces
4 tablespoons butter
2 large onions, grated
1 clove garlic (optional)
2 cups canned tomatoes
1 tablespoon tomato paste*

*Salt and pepper
Water (about 2 cups)
6 medium potatoes, quartered
1 pound peas
1 pound string beans*

Brown chicken in butter with onions and garlic, if desired. Add tomatoes, tomato paste, salt and pepper, and water. Bring to a boil,
add vegetables, cover, and cook until tender. *6 servings*

ROAST DUCKLING *Papaki Psito*

1 ready-to-cook duckling, (5–6 pounds)	*Oregano*
	1 lemon, juice of
Salt and pepper	

Rub duckling with salt and pepper and oregano. Sprinkle with lemon juice. Place on rack in roasting pan and roast in a slow oven (325 degrees) for about 2 hours or until crisp and tender. *4 servings*

ROAST CHICKEN OR TURKEY *Kotopoulo–Galopoulo tou Fournou*

1 ready-to-cook roasting chicken or turkey	*Stuffing*
	1 lemon, juice of
Salt and pepper	*½ cup melted butter*

Have chicken or turkey at room temperature. Rub inside and out with salt and pepper. Stuff with one of the following stuffings and truss with string or skewers. Rub skin with juice of half the lemon and brush with melted butter. Roast in a 325-degree oven. Add remaining lemon juice to remaining butter and baste with the mixture every ½ hour until the fowl is tender.

STUFFINGS FOR TURKEY OR LARGE ROASTING CHICKEN
Yemises Galopoulou–Kotas

Stuffing #1:

2 pounds chestnuts	*¼ pound butter*
1 pound walnuts	*1 egg*
1 pound blanched almonds	*Salt and pepper to taste*
Gizzard and heart of fowl	*1 teaspoon cinnamon*
2 pounds chopped beef	

Roast chestnuts, shell, and break nuts into pieces. Set aside. Grind walnuts and almonds with the gizzard and heart. Add chopped beef and brown the mixture lightly in butter. Add broken-up chestnuts and brown for a few minutes longer. Cool mixture, add egg, salt and pepper, and cinnamon and mix well. Stuff bird and truss.

Stuffing ✷2:

1 onion, grated
1 pound ground beef
¼ pound butter
1 pound cooked chestnuts
   broken into large pieces
½ cup raisins
Salt and pepper to taste

1 teaspoon tomato paste
1 cup walnuts or blanched
   almonds, chopped
½ cup pitted, quartered prunes
¼ pound pignolia nuts
1 teaspoon cinnamon

Brown onion and beef in the butter. Add remaining ingredients and mix well. Stuff bird and truss.

Stuffing ✷3:

2 onions, finely chopped
¼ pound butter
1 pound ground chuck
Liver of the fowl, chopped
4 ounces red wine (½ cup)
1 1-pound can whole tomatoes
2 tablespoons tomato paste
Parsley and dill, chopped

Salt and pepper
1 cup raw rice
2 cups water
½ pound cooked chestnuts
   broken into large pieces
¼ pound pignolia nuts
½ cup raisins
1 apple, sliced

Brown onions in butter. Add meat and liver and brown for a few minutes longer. Add wine, tomatoes, tomato paste, parsley and dill, and salt and pepper. Cover and simmer until meat is cooked. Add rice, water, nuts, and fruit, cover, and continue to cook until liquid is absorbed by the rice. Stuff bird and truss.

Stuffing ✷4:

Gizzard, heart, and liver of the
   fowl
2 boxes (6-ounces net weight)
   zwieback
3 pounds chestnuts
1 pound butter
1 onion, chopped

4 stalks celery, chopped
5 cups water
Cinnamon
Allspice
Clove
Salt and pepper
4 eggs, lightly beaten

Parboil gizzard, heart, and liver until almost tender and chop. Roll zwieback into fine crumbs. Cook chestnuts in boiling water to cover until tender, shell while hot, and break meat into large pieces. Divide butter into four parts. In one part butter brown chestnuts and transfer to a large kettle. In second part of the butter brown onions and celery and add to kettle. Brown chopped gizzard, heart, and liver in the third part of butter and add to kettle. Finally, brown zwieback crumbs in the last part of the butter and add to kettle. Gradually stir in water. Season to taste with cinnamon, allspice, clove, and salt and pepper. Stir in eggs and cook mixture over low heat, stirring constantly, until thoroughly blended. Stuff turkey and truss. For a large chicken, use only half the ingredients.

Stuffing #5:

2 onions, chopped
¼ pound butter
Liver and heart of fowl,
    chopped
½ pound chopped meat
Mint and parsley, chopped

Dash each cinnamon and clove
Salt and pepper to taste
1 teaspoon tomato paste
1¼ cups water
½ cup raw rice

Sauté onions in butter until golden. Add liver and heart and the chopped meat and continue to sauté until meat is browned. Add herbs, spices, and salt and pepper. Dilute tomato paste in water and add. Bring liquid to a boil. Add rice, cover, and cook until water is absorbed by the rice. Stuff fowl and truss.

MEATS

MEAT

Lamb is the staple meat of Greece, and there are endless interesting and delicious ways of preparing it, unknown today, for the most part, in America.

Spit-roasted spring lamb is traditional for the Easter feast that follows the long Lenten fasting, and the entrails are used to make the Easter soup, mageritsa,* and kokoretsi.* The lamb is often served with pilaf,* and is sometimes stuffed with *pilaf* before it is roasted. Suckling pig is also spit-roasted over charcoal, although pork itself is not too popular. Occasionally it is stuffed before roasting with a fascinating filling of crumbed feta cheese* mixed with chopped parsley and subtly flavored with one of Greece's favorite herbs, oregano.

However, the majority of meat dishes in Greece are prepared in stews or casseroles. Cubed meat is simmered until tender with every kind of vegetable conceivable and served with the famous Greek egg-and-lemon sauce (avgolemono).* And ground lamb or beef is used to stuff vegetables, grape leaves, and cabbage leaves, and is combined with eggplant in the famous Grecian moussaka.*

Rabbit or beef stewed with onions in a highly seasoned sauce is called stefado,* and there is an interesting legend concerning this dish. Some bandits hiding on the outskirts of a mountain village smelled the mouth-watering aroma of a rabbit simmering in a pot on the outdoor stove of a near-by cottage. The chief ordered his men to fetch the pot of stew and proceeded to eat the entire dish while his fellow bandits looked on hungrily. The dish was so delicious that the bandit chief spared the village from plunder.

Throughout the meat chapter in this book you will find a repetition of tomatoes, onions, garlic, parsley, oregano, and cinnamon. These basic ingredients are the key to the savory, aromatic meat dishes of Greece, which could do much to add blessed relief to the everlasting roasts, steaks, and chops served too frequently on American tables.

ROAST MEATS

TRADITIONAL LEG OF LAMB   *Arni Psito*

1 leg of young spring lamb   *4 tablespoons butter, melted*
2–3 cloves garlic   *1 lemon, juice of*
Salt and pepper   *2 cups hot water*

Wash leg of lamb. Slit with a sharp knife in various places on both sides of lamb. Slice garlic thinly and insert the slices in slits made in lamb. Season with salt and pepper and brush with melted butter. Squeeze lemon juice over lamb and place in roasting pan, fat side up. Roast at 450 degrees for about ½ hour. Lower heat to moderate (350 degrees) and add hot water. Roast for about 3 hours, adding more water if needed. Remove most of the fat from liquid remaining in pan and serve the lamb with its natural juices. *8 servings*

ROAST LAMB WITH POTATOES   *Arni Psito me Patates*

1 leg of young spring lamb   *20 small potatoes, peeled*
2–3 cloves garlic   *Salt*
Salt and pepper   *2 tablespoons tomato paste*
4 tablespoons butter, melted   *2 cups hot water*
1 lemon, juice of

Prepare lamb as for TRADITIONAL LEG OF LAMB, with garlic, salt and pepper, butter, and lemon juice. While lamb is browning in a 450-degree oven, sprinkle potatoes with salt, rub with tomato paste, and let stand for a few minutes. Add potatoes to the baking pan with the water and lower oven temperature to 350 degrees. Turn and baste the potatoes occasionally during the roasting period. When lamb is done, remove to hot serving platter and keep warm. Increase oven temperature to 425 degrees and brown potatoes for 20 minutes longer. *8 servings*

ROAST RACK OF LAMB WITH STUFFING *Arnaki Yemisto*

½ cup raw rice
5–6 tablespoons butter
1¼ cups water or bouillon
½ pound lamb liver
½ pound lamb kidney
1 onion, finely chopped
¼ cup currants or raisins

¼ cup pignolia nuts
Dill and parsley, chopped
Salt and pepper to taste
1 4-pound rack of lamb
1 lemon, juice of
4 tablespoons melted butter

Sauté rice in 3 tablespoons of the butter until golden. Add water or bouillon, cover, and simmer until rice is cooked. Set aside. Cut liver and kidney into small pieces. In frying pan melt remaining 2 to 3 tablespoons butter and in it sauté chopped onion until soft. Add liver and kidneys and sauté until tender, stirring constantly. Cool and cut meat into very small pieces. Add cooked rice, currants or raisins, nuts, dill and parsley, and salt and pepper and mix well.

Season the lamb with salt and pepper, stuff with the rice mixture, and tie. Rub meat with lemon juice and melted butter and place in baking pan. Bake in a 350-degree oven, basting occasionally, for about 2 hours, or until meat is done.

To serve: Remove stuffing and slice meat. Arrange meat on serving platter with the stuffing. Make pan gravy and pour over the meat. *6 servings*

Note: This recipe may be made with boned leg of lamb, which can be stuffed and rolled. Roast in a moderate oven about 30 minutes per pound or until done. Arrange on platter and slice. Serve pan gravy separately.

ROAST LAMB WITH ARTICHOKES *Arni Psito me Anginares*

6 artichokes
Cold water, salted
6 lemons, juice of
2 tablespoons flour
4-pound lamb roast

Salt and pepper
1 tablespoon oregano
½ cup (one stick) butter
2 cups water
Parsley sprigs

Remove tough outer leaves of the artichokes and cut off part of the stems. Cut ½ to 1 inch off tips of remaining leaves. Rub cut stems of artichokes with a cut lemon and cut in half lengthwise. Rub cut surfaces with lemon. Cut and scrape the fuzz or choke from the artichoke hearts. Place the artichokes in a bowl of cold salted water to cover into which the juice of 2 lemons and the flour have been stirred. This solution helps keep the artichokes green. Soak at least ½ hour.

Preheat oven to 450 degrees. Rub meat with salt and pepper, oregano, and the juice of 1 lemon. Roast 20 minutes and reduce heat to 350 degrees. Spread half the butter over the meat, add 1 cup of water to the roasting pan, and cook 15 minutes longer. Add remaining butter and water to the pan and continue cooking for 30 minutes or until meat is done to taste. Baste occasionally with pan drippings. If necessary, add more water. There should be 2 cups of liquid drippings in the pan when the meat is done. Transfer the lamb to a warm platter and keep warm. Add the artichokes to the roasting pan. Bake them, cut side down, 1 hour or until tender but not overcooked. Baste occasionally while cooking. Arrange the artichokes around the lamb and garnish with parsley. *6 servings*

Note: To reduce cooking time, the artichokes may be parboiled before baking. Or, if roasting pan is large enough, artichokes may be added to the pan with the lamb after the temperature is reduced to 350 degrees.

ROAST LAMB WITH ASPARAGUS   *Arni Psito me Asparangi*

1 leg of lamb	1 1-pound can plum tomatoes
2–3 cloves garlic	Oregano
4 tablespoons butter, melted	Salt and pepper
1 lemon, juice of	2–3 cans asparagus

Roast leg of lamb according to TRADITIONAL LEG OF LAMB recipe. When half cooked, add plum tomatoes, oregano, and salt and pepper. Bake for 20 minutes. Add asparagus along with some of the liquid from the cans, if necessary, and bake 20 minutes longer or until meat is cooked to taste. *8 servings*

ROAST LAMB WITH ORZO   *Giouvetsi*

Leg or shoulder of lamb	1 6-ounce can tomato paste
1–2 cloves garlic	4–6 cups boiling water
Salt and pepper	1 pound orzo,* rice, or macaroni
1 onion, sliced	Parmesan cheese and/or feta or
Lemon juice	kasseri cheese,* cubed

Prepare lamb and season to taste. Insert pieces of garlic in slits made in meat with a sharp knife and sprinkle with salt and pepper.

Place in baking pan, add onion slices, and bake in 425-degree oven for 30 minutes. Reduce oven temperature to 350 degrees. Baste meat with lemon juice and return to oven until meat is done and well browned. Remove meat and onions from baking pan and keep warm.

Add tomato paste and boiling water to pan drippings. Use 4 cups water for rice, 6 or more for *pasta*. Sprinkle rice or *pasta* in baking pan slowly and return to oven. Stir occasionally. When rice or *pasta* is cooked, remove from oven and allow to stand, covered with a towel, for a few minutes. Serve with grated Parmesan cheese and/or cubes of *feta* or *kasseri* cheese. Arrange on platter with meat and onions. *8 servings*

Note: Onion and garlic may be omitted, if desired. Pasta may be parboiled, drained, and added to baking pan with small amount of water.

LAMB SURPRISE *Arni tis Tihis*

Leg of lamb	*Celery*
Garlic, thinly sliced	*Potatoes*
*Feta cheese**	*Butter*
*Kasseri or kefalotiri cheese**	*Lemon juice*
Small carrots	*Salt and pepper*
Small white onions	

Cube meat from leg of lamb in 4- to 5-inch serving pieces. Cut incisions in meat and insert slivers of garlic. Place each piece of meat on a large square of heavy-duty aluminum foil. Add one 1-inch cube of each cheese, 1 small carrot, 1 small onion, 1 piece of celery, and 1 medium potato, pared, halved, and rubbed with butter. Add a squeeze of lemon juice and salt and pepper. Fold the foil in double fold at top and seal like a package. Arrange packages close together in a baking pan and bake 2 to 2½ hours in 350-degree oven. Serve each foil package, sealed, on dinner plate and let each guest open his own. *8 servings*

ROAST LAMB HEADS *Kefalakia Arniou Riganata*

Small lamb heads	Lemon juice
Salt and pepper	Olive oil
Oregano	Small potatoes, peeled

Have butcher split the lamb heads in half. Tie the heads together to keep the brains intact and soak in cold water for several hours, changing water frequently to remove all the blood. Remove string and place the heads in a baking pan, cut side up. Rub with salt and pepper, oregano, and lemon juice and sprinkle generously with olive oil. Roast in a hot 425-degree oven for 20 minutes. Reduce oven temperature to 375 degrees, add potatoes, and bake for 1 hour longer, basting frequently with liquid in pan.

LAMB CHOPS A LA HASAPIKA *Païdakia Hasapika*

5–6 shoulder lamb chops	Salt and pepper
2 medium onions, sliced	1 1-pound can plum tomatoes
Oregano	New potatoes

Place lamb chops in baking pan and add onions, oregano, salt and pepper, and tomatoes. Bake in a moderate 350-degree oven for about 1 hour, turning chops once. Add small peeled new potatoes and bake 30 minutes longer or until potatoes are cooked, adding a little water if necessary. *4 servings*

ROAST PORK *Hirino Psito*

Fresh ham or loin of pork roast	Lemon juice
Garlic	Water
Salt and pepper	1 cup dry white wine

Cut slits in meat with a sharp knife and add slivers of garlic. Rub meat with salt and pepper and lemon juice. Brown in a hot 450-degree oven. Add a little water and skim off fat. Lower oven to moderate, 350 degrees, and add white wine. Bake until meat is well done, allowing total baking time of 45 minutes per pound of meat. Add additional water for gravy if necessary.

ROAST LOIN OF PORK *Hirino Psito Riganato*

Loin of pork	*Oregano*
Salt and pepper	*Small potatoes or potato cubes*
Lemon juice	*2 cups water*

Rub loin of pork with salt and pepper, lemon juice, and oregano. Bake in a slow 350-degree oven until meat is well done, allowing 45 minutes per pound for a small 3 to 4 pound roast, 20 minutes per pound for a whole loin. Add potatoes or potato cubes and water 1 hour before meat is done. Baste often.

ROAST SUCKLING PIG *Ghourounaki Psito*

1 suckling pig, 10–12 pounds	*½ cup olive oil*
Salt and pepper	*¼ cup lemon juice*
2 lemons, halved	

Carefully clean a small suckling pig, wash inside and out with cold water, and dry thoroughly. Rub inside and out with salt and pepper and cut lemons, saving 1 of the lemon halves. Allow to stand for about 1 hour.

Pull front legs of the piglet forward and tie together. Wedge the mouth open with a small piece of wood. Rub entire pig generously with olive oil and lemon juice, mixed.

Place pig on a rack in roasting pan and roast in a 425- to 450-degree oven for 30 minutes. Reduce temperature to 325 degrees and continue roasting for about 4 to 5 hours. Baste often, using a lemon half dipped in pan drippings as baster. To serve, untie legs, remove wedge of wood from mouth, and put a shiny red apple in mouth.

A suckling pig prepared as above may also be skewered and cooked over charcoal. Allow 4 to 5 hours cooking time and turn often. *6 servings*

STUFFINGS FOR ROAST SUCKLING PIG

A suckling pig may be roasted without stuffing; however, if a stuffing is desired, any favorite may be used, or perhaps one of the following:

Feta Cheese Stuffing:

> 2 pounds feta cheese,*
> crumbled
> ½ cup parsley, chopped

Prepare piglet as above, rubbing it inside and out with salt and pepper, a little oregano, lemon juice, and olive oil.

Stuff piglet with the cheese mixed with parsley. Sew or skewer opening closed and roast as directed.

Apple Stuffing:

> ¼ cup butter
> 2 quarts tart apples, diced
> ¼ cup brown sugar
>
> 1 teaspoon cinnamon
> 1 tablespoon grated lemon rind
> 2 cups dry bread cubes

Heat butter in a large, heavy skillet; add apples, sugar, cinnamon, and lemon rind. Stir over low heat just until apples are tender but not mushy. Add bread cubes and toss together lightly. Stuff piglet and roast as directed.

SHISH KEBAB *Souvlakia*

> Leg of lamb
> 1 cup olive oil
> ⅓ cup lemon juice
> ½ cup wine
> Salt and pepper
> Oregano
> 1–2 cloves garlic, chopped
>
> 1–2 bay leaves
> Tomatoes, quartered
> Onions, quartered and separated
> Green peppers, cut in 1-inch
>   squares
> Mushroom caps (optional)

Cut a leg of lamb into 1- to 2-inch cubes. Combine olive oil, lemon juice, and wine and pour this marinade over the meat. Sprinkle with salt and pepper, oregano, and garlic. Add 1 or 2 bay leaves and place quartered tomatoes and onion pieces on top of meat. Weigh down with a heavy plate, cover, and refrigerate overnight.

Skewer meat, alternating with tomatoes, onions, green peppers, and mushroom caps, if desired. Cook skewers over charcoal (or in oven broiler), basting and turning occasionally, for about 20–25 minutes or until cooked to taste. 8 *servings*

KOKORETSI

1 lamb membrane
1 lamb liver
1 lamb lung
1 lamb heart
1 dozen lamb sweetbreads
  (optional)

2–3 bunches scallions, finely
  chopped, including tender
  green part
½ cup dill, finely chopped
Salt and pepper to taste
½ cup raw rice

Put the lamb membrane into cold water to soak.

Cover the liver, lung, and heart with boiling water and boil for about 5 minutes. Drain and grind through fine blade of a meat chopper. Cut each sweetbread into 3 pieces and add to the ground meat. Add scallions, dill, salt and pepper, and rice, and mix well. Turn mixture into a deep casserole. Remove the membrane from the cold water and trim off as much of the fatty tissue as possible. Cover the mixture in the casserole with the membrane, tucking it under the mixture on the bottom of the casserole. Patch any torn areas of membrane with additional pieces. Bake the *kokoretsi* in a medium 350-degree oven for about 45 minutes or until puffed and golden brown. Serve warm with a spoon. *6–8 servings*

KOKORETSI ON A SPIT *Kokoretsi tis Souvlas*

Heart, liver, kidney, sweetbread,
  and intestines of a young
  lamb
Salt and pepper

Oregano
Lemon juice
Olive oil

Wash the entrails thoroughly. Wash the intestines inside and out. Parboil the heart, liver, kidney, and sweetbread, then drain and chop coarsely along with a small portion of the intestines. Season with salt and pepper, oregano, and lemon juice. Mold the mixture into a thick, long "sausage," winding it with remaining intestine to keep mixture together. Skewer on a spit and grill slowly for several hours, basting with olive oil and lemon juice. When ready to serve, cut the *kokoretsi tis souvlas* into slices. *6–8 servings*

VARIATION: After parboiling the internal meats, cut in pieces the size of walnuts, season as above, and skewer on a spit. Cover meats with a piece of membrane soaked and trimmed as instructed in recipe for KOKORETSI. Wind intestines around membrane-covered spit and grill slowly for several hours, basting as instructed above.

MEAT CASSEROLES

LAMB WITH VEGETABLES–Basic Recipe   *Arni Entrada*

3 pounds lean shoulder of lamb	*1 cup water*
2–3 tablespoons butter	*Vegetable*
2–3 onions, chopped	*Salt and pepper*
1 cup tomato sauce	*Seasonings, if desired*

Cut lamb into 3-inch cubes. Melt butter in a saucepan or casserole, add meat and onions and brown well over moderate heat. Add tomato sauce, water, vegetable, salt and pepper, and seasonings. Bring mixture to a boil, cover, and simmer for 1½ to 2 hours or until meat is tender. Add more water if necessary. *4–6 servings*

Note: If preferred, fresh tomatoes, canned whole tomatoes, or 2 tablespoons tomato paste may be substituted for tomato sauce in any of these recipes.

LAMB WITH ARTICHOKES, AVGOLEMONO
Anginares Kreas Avgolemono

12 small artichokes	*2–3 onions, chopped*
Cold water, salted	*2 cups water*
5 lemons	*Salt and pepper*
4 tablespoons flour	*Fresh dill, chopped*
3 pounds lean shoulder of lamb	*5 scallions, chopped*
2–3 tablespoons butter	*3 eggs*

Remove the tough outer leaves of the artichokes and cut off part of the stem. Cut ½ to 1 inch off tips of remaining leaves. Rub artichokes with a cut lemon and cut in half lengthwise. Rub cut surfaces with cut lemon. Cut and scrape the fuzz or choke from the artichoke hearts. Place the vegetables in a bowl of cold salted water to which the juice of 2 lemons and 2 tablespoons of the flour have been added. Soak for at least 1 hour. If desired, artichokes may be sautéed in butter before adding to meat.

Cut lamb into 3-inch cubes. Melt butter in a saucepan or casserole, add meat and onions, and brown well over moderate heat. Add water, salt and pepper, dill, and the juice of 1 lemon. Bring mixture to a boil, cover, and simmer for 1 hour. Drain and add artichokes and chopped scallions and continue cooking for 1 hour or until meat and vegetables are done. Remove from heat and allow casserole to cool while preparing *avgolemono* sauce: Beat eggs until light; add remaining 2 tablespoons of flour and juice of 1½ lemons and mix well. Very slowly add liquid from casserole to egg mixture, stirring constantly, until about 1 cup of the hot liquid has been added. Pour into stew slowly, shaking pan until sauce mixes with liquid in casserole. Serve immediately. *6 servings*

LAMB WITH BROCCOLI, AVGOLEMONO
Kreas me Brokola Avgolemono

3 pounds lean shoulder of lamb	2 bunches broccoli
2–3 tablespoons butter	3 eggs
2–3 onions, chopped	2 tablespoons flour
2 cups water	1½ lemons, juice of
Salt and pepper	

Cut lamb into cubes. Melt butter in a saucepan or casserole, add meat and onions, and brown well over moderate heat. Add water and salt and pepper, cover, and simmer for 30 minutes. Wash and drain broccoli. Add broccoli to meat and continue cooking over low heat for about 1 hour or until meat and vegetables are tender. Remove from heat and allow casserole to cool a little while preparing *avgolemono* sauce: Beat eggs until light, add flour and lemon juice, and mix well. Very slowly stir in about 1 cup liquid from the stew. Then pour egg mixture slowly into stew, shaking pan until sauce mixes with the stew. Serve immediately. *6 servings*

LAMB WITH BRUSSELS SPROUTS *Kreas me Lahanakia*

3 pounds lean shoulder of lamb	2 pounds Brussels sprouts, cleaned
2–3 tablespoons butter	Salt and pepper
2–3 onions, chopped	Parsley, chopped
1 cup tomato sauce	Lemon wedges
1 cup water	

Cut lamb into 3-inch cubes. Melt butter in a saucepan or casserole; add meat and onions and brown well over moderate heat. Add tomato sauce, water, Brussels sprouts, salt and pepper, and parsley. Bring mixture to a boil, cover, and simmer for 1½ to 2 hours or until meat is tender. Add more water if necessary. Serve with lemon wedges. *6 servings*

LAMB WITH CABBAGE *Kreas me Lahano*

3 pounds lean shoulder of lamb
2–3 tablespoons butter
2–3 onions, chopped
1 cup tomato sauce
1 cup water

1 large head of cabbage, cut into wedges
Salt and pepper
Lemon wedges

Cut lamb into 3-inch cubes. Melt butter in a saucepan or casserole, add meat and onions, and brown well over moderate heat. Add tomato sauce, water, cabbage, and salt and pepper. Bring mixture to a boil, cover, and simmer for 1½ to 2 hours or until meat is tender. Add more water if necessary. Serve with lemon wedges. *6 servings*

LAMB WITH CABBAGE, AVGOLEMONO
Kreas me Lahano Avgolemono

3 pounds lean shoulder of lamb
2–3 tablespoons butter
2–3 onions, chopped
2 cups water
1 large head of cabbage, cut into wedges

Salt and pepper
3 eggs
2 tablespoons flour
1½ lemons, juice of

Cut lamb into 3-inch cubes. Melt butter in a saucepan or casserole; add meat and onions and brown well over moderate heat. Add water, cabbage, and salt and pepper. Bring mixture to a boil, cover, and simmer for 1½ to 2 hours or until meat is tender. Add more water if necessary. When meat and cabbage are cooked, remove casserole from heat and allow to cool while preparing *avgolemono* sauce: Beat eggs until light, add flour and lemon juice, and mix well. Very slowly add liquid from stew, stirring constantly, until about 1 cup of the hot liquid has been added. Pour into stew slowly, shaking pan until sauce mixes with liquid in casserole. Serve immediately. *6 servings*

LAMB WITH CAULIFLOWER, AVGOLEMONO
Kreas me Kounopidi Avgolemono

3 pounds lean shoulder of lamb	Salt and pepper
2–3 tablespoons butter	3 eggs
2–3 onions, chopped	2 tablespoons flour
2 heads cauliflower	1½ lemons, juice of
2 cups water	

Cut lamb into 3-inch cubes. Melt butter in a saucepan or casserole, add meat and onions, and brown well over moderate heat. Cut cauliflower into flowerets and add to casserole with water and salt and pepper. Bring mixture to a boil, cover, and simmer for 1½ to 2 hours or until meat is tender. Remove from heat and allow casserole to cool while preparing *avgolemono* sauce: Beat eggs until light, add flour and lemon juice, and mix well. Very slowly add liquid from stew, stirring constantly, until about 1 cup of the hot liquid has been added. Pour sauce over stew slowly, shaking pan until sauce mixes with liquid in casserole. Serve immediately. *6 servings*

LAMB WITH CELERY   *Kreas me Selino*

3 pounds lean shoulder of lamb	1 cup water
2–3 tablespoons butter	Salt and pepper
2–3 onions, chopped	3 bunches celery
1 cup tomato sauce	

Cut lamb into 3-inch cubes. Melt butter in a saucepan or casserole, add meat and onions, and brown well over moderate heat. Add tomato sauce, water, and salt and pepper. Save hearts of celery for salad. Scrub and scrape remaining stalks and cut into 2- or 3-inch pieces. Add celery to meat. Bring mixture to a boil, cover, and simmer for 1½ to 2 hours or until meat is tender. *6 servings*

LAMB WITH CELERY, AVGOLEMONO   *Kreas me Selino Avgolemono*

3 pounds lean shoulder of lamb	Salt and pepper
2–3 tablespoons butter	3 bunches celery
2–3 onions, chopped	3 eggs
2 cups water	2 tablespoons flour
Fresh dill, chopped	1½ lemons, juice of

Cut lamb into 3-inch cubes. Melt butter in a saucepan or casserole, add meat and onions, and brown well over moderate heat. Add water, dill, and salt and pepper. Save hearts of celery for salad. Scrub and scrape remaining stalks and cut into 2- or 3-inch pieces. Add celery to meat. Bring mixture to a boil, cover, and simmer for 1½ to 2 hours or until meat is tender. Remove from heat and allow casserole to cool while preparing *avgolemono* sauce: Beat eggs until light, add flour and lemon juice, and mix well. Very slowly add liquid from stew, stirring constantly, until about 1 cup of the hot liquid has been added. Pour sauce into stew slowly, shaking pan until sauce mixes with liquid in casserole. Serve immediately. *6 servings*

LAMB WITH CELERY AND LEEKS, AVGOLEMONO
Kreas me Selino ke Prasa Avgolemono

Follow recipe for LAMB WITH CELERY, AVGOLEMONO, but use 1½ bunches celery and 1½ bunches leeks instead of all celery. Wash leeks thoroughly and cut into 2-inch pieces, using as much of the tender green portion as desired. *6 servings*

LAMB WITH DANDELION GREENS *Kreas me Radikia*

3 pounds lean shoulder of lamb	*1 cup water*
2–3 tablespoons butter	*Salt and pepper*
2–3 onions, chopped	*2 pounds dandelion greens*
1 cup tomato sauce	

Cut lamb into 3-inch cubes. Melt butter in a saucepan or casserole, add meat and onions, and brown well over moderate heat. Add tomato sauce, water, and salt and pepper. Wash dandelion greens thoroughly. Add to meat and bring liquid to a boil. Cover and simmer for 1½ to 2 hours or until meat is tender. *4–6 servings*

LAMB WITH EGGPLANT *Kreas me Melitzana*

3 pounds lean shoulder of lamb	*1 cup water*
2–3 tablespoons butter	*Salt and pepper*
2–3 onions, chopped	*2–3 large eggplants*
1 cup tomato sauce	*1 clove garlic or garlic powder*

Cut lamb into 3-inch cubes. Melt butter in a saucepan or casserole, add meat and onions, and brown well over moderate heat. Add tomato sauce, water, and salt and pepper. Bring to a boil, cover, and simmer for 1 hour. Peel eggplant and cut into 2-inch cubes. After meat has cooked for 1 hour add eggplant and garlic and continue cooking for 30 minutes or until meat and vegetables are done. *6 servings*

LAMB WITH ESCAROLE, AVGOLEMONO
Kreas me Andithia Avgolemono

3 pounds lean shoulder of lamb	Salt and pepper
2–3 tablespoons butter	3 eggs
2–3 onions, chopped	2 tablespoons flour
2 pounds escarole	1½ lemons, juice of
1 cup water	

Cut lamb into 3-inch cubes. Melt butter in a saucepan or casserole, add meat and onions, and brown well over moderate heat. Wash and cut escarole into pieces. Add to meat with water and salt and pepper. Bring mixture to a boil, cover, and simmer for 1½ to 2 hours or until meat is tender. Add more water if necessary. When meat and vegetable are cooked, remove casserole from heat and allow to cool slightly while preparing *avgolemono* sauce: Beat eggs until light, add flour and lemon juice, and mix well. Very slowly add liquid from stew, stirring constantly, until about 1 cup of the hot liquid has been added. Slowly pour egg mixture into stew, shaking pan until sauce mixes with liquid in casserole. Serve immediately. *4–6 servings*

LAMB WITH FAVA BEANS   *Kreas me Koukia Freska*

3 pounds shoulder of lamb	Fresh dill, chopped
2–3 tablespoons butter	Fresh or dried mint
2–3 onions, chopped	Salt and pepper
2–3 pounds fava beans*	1 cup tomato sauce (optional)
2 cups water	

Cut lamb into 3-inch cubes. Melt butter in a saucepan or casserole, add meat and onions, and brown well over moderate heat. Wash and shell *fava* beans. Any tender outer skins may be added with beans to casserole. Add water, beans, dill, mint, salt and pepper, and tomato sauce, if desired. Bring mixture to a boil, cover, and simmer for 1½ to 2 hours or until meat is tender, adding more water if needed. *6 servings*

LAMB WITH LEEKS, AVGOLEMONO
Kreas me Prasa Avgolemono

3 pounds lean shoulder of lamb
2–3 tablespoons butter
2–3 onions, chopped
2 bunches leeks
2 cups water

Salt and pepper
3 eggs
2 tablespoons flour
1½ lemons, juice of

Cut lamb into 3-inch cubes. Melt butter in a saucepan or casserole, add meat and onions, and brown well over moderate heat. Wash leeks thoroughly and cut into 2-inch pieces. Add water, leeks, and salt and pepper to casserole. Bring mixture to a boil, cover, and simmer for 1½ to 2 hours or until meat is tender. Remove from heat and allow to cool slightly while preparing *avgolemono* sauce: Beat eggs until light, add flour and lemon juice, and mix well. Very slowly add liquid from stew, stirring constantly, until about 1 cup of the hot liquid has been added. Pour egg mixture into stew slowly, shaking pan until sauce mixes with liquid in casserole. Serve immediately. *6 servings*

LAMB WITH LETTUCE HEARTS *Kreas me Maroulia*

3 pounds lean shoulder of lamb
2–3 tablespoons butter
2 onions, chopped
2 cups water
Salt and pepper

3 pounds lettuce hearts (about 4–5)
Dill, chopped
1 bunch scallions, coarsely chopped
AVGOLEMONO SAUCE (*optional*)

Cut lamb into cubes. Melt butter in a saucepan or casserole, add meat and onions, and brown well over moderate heat. Add water and salt and pepper, bring to a boil, cover, and simmer for 1 hour. Meanwhile cover lettuce hearts with boiling water and let stand while meat is cooking. When meat is tender, add lettuce, dill, and scallions. Bring to a boil and simmer for 15 minutes longer. *Avgolemono* sauce may be added if desired. *4–5 servings*

LAMB WITH OKRA *Kreas me Bamyes*

3 pounds lean shoulder of lamb	1 cup tomato sauce
2–3 tablespoons butter	1 cup water
2–3 onions, chopped	Parsley, chopped
2 pounds okra or 2 packages	Salt and pepper
frozen okra, thawed	½ teaspoon cinnamon (optional)

Cut lamb into 3-inch cubes. Melt butter in a saucepan or casserole, add meat and onions, and brown well over moderate heat. Trim okra by removing cone-shaped portions at top. Add tomato sauce, water, okra, parsley, salt and pepper, and cinnamon, if desired, to casserole. Bring mixture to a boil, cover, and simmer for 1½ to 2 hours or until meat is tender. *6 servings*

LAMB WITH PEAS *Kreas me Bizelia*

3 pounds lean shoulder of lamb	Fresh or dried mint
2–3 tablespoons butter	½ teaspoon sugar
2–3 onions, chopped	Salt and pepper
1 cup tomato sauce	3 pounds peas or 3 packages
1 cup water	frozen peas, thawed

Cut lamb into 3-inch cubes. Melt butter in a saucepan or casserole, add meat and onions, and brown well over moderate heat. Add tomato sauce, water, mint, sugar, and salt and pepper. Bring mixture to a boil, cover, and simmer for 1 hour. Wash and shell peas. After meat has cooked for 1 hour, add peas to casserole and continue cooking for 30 minutes longer. *6 servings*

LAMB WITH POTATOES *Kreas me Patates*

3 pounds lean shoulder of lamb	6–8 potatoes, peeled and
2–3 tablespoons butter	quartered
2–3 onions, chopped	1 teaspoon cinnamon
1 cup tomato sauce	Salt and pepper
1 cup water	

Cut lamb into 3-inch cubes. Melt butter in a saucepan or casserole, add meat and onions, and brown well over moderate heat. Add tomato sauce, water, potatoes, cinnamon, and salt and pepper. Bring mixture to a boil, cover, and simmer for 1½ to 2 hours or until meat is tender. *6 servings*

LAMB WITH SPINACH *Kreas me Spanaki*

3 pounds lean shoulder of lamb	*1 cup water*
2–3 tablespoons butter	*Salt and pepper*
2–3 onions, chopped	*3 pounds spinach*
1 cup tomato sauce	

Cut lamb into 3-inch cubes. Melt butter in a saucepan or casserole, add meat and onions, and brown well over moderate heat. Add tomato sauce, water, and salt and pepper. Bring mixture to a boil, cover, and simmer for 1 hour. Wash spinach thoroughly. Remove any tough stalks. After meat has cooked for 1 hour, add spinach and continue cooking for 15 to 20 minutes longer. *6 servings*

LAMB WITH SPINACH, AVGOLEMONO
Kreas me Spanaki Avgolemono

3 pounds lean shoulder of lamb	*3 pounds spinach*
2–3 tablespoons butter	*3 eggs*
2–3 onions, chopped	*2 tablespoons flour*
1 cup water	*1½ lemons, juice of*
Salt and pepper	

Cut lamb into 3-inch cubes. Melt butter in a saucepan or casserole, add meat and onions, and brown well over moderate heat. Add water and salt and pepper. Bring mixture to a boil, cover, and simmer for 1 hour. Wash spinach thoroughly. Remove any tough stalks. After meat has cooked for 1 hour, add spinach and continue cooking for 15 to 20 minutes. Remove from heat and allow casserole to cool slightly while preparing *avgolemono* sauce: Beat eggs until light, add flour and lemon juice, and mix well. Very slowly add liquid from stew, stirring constantly, until about 1 cup of the hot liquid has been added. Pour egg mixture into stew slowly, shaking pan until sauce mixes with liquid in casserole. Serve immediately. *6 servings*

LAMB WITH STRING BEANS *Kreas me Fassoulakia Freska*

3 pounds lean shoulder of lamb	*1 cup tomato sauce*
2–3 tablespoons butter	*1 cup water*
2–3 onions, chopped	*Fresh dill or parsley, chopped*
2 pounds string beans	*Salt and pepper*

Cut lamb into 3-inch cubes. Melt butter in a saucepan or casserole, add meat and onions, and brown well over moderate heat. Remove ends and strings from beans and slit lengthwise. Add tomato sauce, water, string beans, dill or parsley, and salt and pepper. Bring mixture to a boil, cover, and simmer for 1½ to 2 hours or until meat is tender. *6 servings*

LAMB WITH ZUCCHINI *Kreas me Kolokithia*

3 pounds lean shoulder of lamb	*1 cup water*
2–3 tablespoons butter	*Parsley, chopped, or oregano*
2–3 onions, chopped	*Salt and pepper*
1 cup tomato sauce	*2 pounds zucchini*

Cut lamb into 3-inch cubes. Melt butter in a saucepan or casserole, add meat and onions, and brown well over moderate heat. Add tomato sauce, water, parsley or oregano, and salt and pepper. Bring mixture to a boil, cover, and simmer for 1 hour. Scrape zucchini and cut into 2- to 3-inch pieces. After meat has cooked for 1 hour, add zucchini to casserole and continue cooking for 30 minutes longer or until meat and vegetable are done. *4–6 servings*

Note: If desired, zucchini may be lightly browned in butter before adding to casserole.

LAMB WITH VEGETABLES *Tourlou*

2 pounds lean lamb, cubed	*1 medium eggplant*
2 onions, chopped	*¼ pound okra*
¼ cup butter	*2 large green peppers*
1½ cups hot water	*½ pound string beans*
3 medium tomatoes	*Salt and pepper*
2 small zucchini	

Cut lamb into 2-inch cubes. Sauté onions in butter in large saucepan or casserole until lightly browned. Add meat and ½ cup water and simmer until nearly tender. While meat is cooking, prepare vegetables as follows: Peel and slice tomatoes and zucchini. Remove lengthwise 1-inch strips of eggplant skin, leaving 1-inch strips of skin between, and cut eggplant into 2-inch segments. Trim okra by removing cone-shaped portions at top. Discard seeds from green peppers and dice peppers. Cut ends of string beans, string if necessary, and slit lengthwise. When meat is nearly tender, add remaining water and salt and pepper; then add beans, zucchini, eggplant, tomatoes, green pepper, and okra in that order. Cover tightly and cook until vegetables are done, about 50 minutes. If necessary, additional hot water may be added during cooking. *6 servings*

MEAT WITH QUINCE   *Kreas me Kydonia*

1–2 onions, finely chopped	*2 cups water*
3 pounds lamb or pork cut into	*4 pounds quince*
cubes	*Salt and pepper*
4 tablespoons butter	*1 tablespoon sugar*

Sauté onions and meat in butter until onions are soft and meat is browned. Add water, bring to a boil, and simmer for about 1 hour or until meat is almost tender. Peel quince and cut into thick slices. Add to meat, with more water if necessary, together with salt and pepper and sugar. Continue to cook until meat is very tender and quince are soft. *6 servings*

LAMB FRICASSEE   *Arnaki Vrasto*

3 pounds lamb shoulder, cubed	*2–3 stalks celery, cut in*
Salt and pepper	*sections*
5–6 potatoes, peeled	*1 cup fide**
5–6 small onions, peeled	*2 eggs*
2–3 carrots, scraped and cut in	*1½ lemons, juice of*
sections	

Cover lamb with water and bring to a boil. Add salt and pepper, cover, and simmer for 30 minutes. Add vegetables, cover, and simmer for 1 hour or until lamb and vegetables are tender. Carefully remove meat and vegetables to a warm platter and keep hot. Strain broth. Add *fide* and additional salt, if necessary, and cook for 10 to 15 minutes or until *fide* is tender. Beat eggs with lemon juice. Very slowly beat in about 1 cup of the hot broth, then add to broth, stirring vigorously, until sauce mixes with the broth.

Serve the sauce mixture first with the *fide* as a soup, then serve the boiled meat and vegetables. *4–6 servings*

LAMB WITH EGGPLANT PUREE *Hunkar Begendi**

½ cup butter
2 pounds leg of lamb, cubed
3 onions, finely grated
2 teaspoons tomato paste
1 cup water
Salt and pepper
2 large eggplants
1 cup cream

1 cup milk
¼ cup butter
Kefalotiri* or Parmesan cheese, grated
½ cup bread crumbs
Parsley, chopped
Green pepper rings, thinly sliced

Melt the ½ cup butter in casserole, add meat and onions, and brown well over moderate heat. Add tomato paste mixed with water and salt and pepper. Bring mixture to a boil, cover, and simmer for 1½ to 2 hours or until meat is done and sauce is thick. Prick eggplants and place whole, with skin on, in a hot oven or broiler. Cook until tender. Strip off charred skins and mash eggplant. Add cream, milk, the ¼ cup butter, and grated cheese. Stir in bread crumbs and correct seasoning. Mix well and heat, stirring constantly, until mixture becomes a thick purée.

To serve *Hunkar Begendi*, place eggplant purée on serving platter. Arrange lamb and sauce (tas kebab*) on top, and garnish with chopped parsley and thinly sliced green pepper rings. *6 servings*

LAMB WITH RICE *Arnaki Atzem Pilafi*

3 pounds lamb—leg, shoulder, or shanks
5–6 tablespoons butter
2 onions, chopped

1 cup tomato purée or 1 cup tomato sauce
2 cups bouillon or water
Salt and pepper
1½ cups rice

Cut meat into bite-size pieces. Melt butter in a casserole, add meat and onions, and brown well over moderate heat. Add tomato, bouillon or water, and salt and pepper. Bring mixture to a boil, cover, and simmer for 45 minutes to 1 hour or until meat is almost tender. Add rice and stir well. Bring to a boil again, cover, and simmer for about 20 minutes or until rice absorbs all the liquid. *6–8 servings*

LAMB IN CASSEROLE *Arni Tas Kebab*

2 pounds leg of lamb	3 onions, thinly sliced
4 tablespoons butter	Parsley, chopped
3 onions, chopped	½ cup dry white wine
2 fresh tomatoes, peeled and chopped, or 1 tablespoon tomato paste	½ cup water
	Salt and pepper

Cut meat into bite-size pieces. Melt butter in a casserole, add meat and chopped onion, and brown well over moderate heat. Add tomato, sliced onions, parsley, wine, water, and salt and pepper. Bring mixture to a boil, cover, and simmer for about 1 hour or until done. Add more water if necessary. *4–6 servings*

ONION STEW WITH BEEF *Stefado*

2–3 pounds lean beef	Salt and pepper
4 tablespoons butter	Water
½ 6-ounce can tomato paste	2 pounds small white onions
1 clove garlic, chopped	1 cup walnut halves
1 bay leaf	Feta cheese*
1–2 tablespoons wine vinegar	

Cut beef into 1-inch cubes and brown in butter in casserole. Add tomato paste, garlic, bay leaf, wine vinegar, salt and pepper, and enough water to cover. Bring to a boil, cover tightly, and simmer for 1½ to 2 hours or until meat is tender. Remove meat from casserole and add white onions to sauce remaining in casserole. Bring to a boil again, cover, and simmer for 20 minutes or until onions are cooked. Return meat to casserole, add walnut halves, and continue to simmer for 15 to 20 minutes. During last 5 minutes of cooking add cubes of *feta* cheese. *4–6 servings*

Alternate method of preparation: After browning meat the remaining ingredients, with the exception of the walnuts and *feta* cheese, are added immediately. Bring mixture to a boil, cover, and simmer until meat and onions are cooked. Walnuts and *feta* cheese are added in last 5 minutes of cooking time.

BEEF STEW *Vothino Yahni*

3 pounds beef round or chuck
4 pounds small white onions
⅓ cup olive oil
3 tablespoons wine vinegar
Salt and pepper

3 bay leaves
2 cloves garlic
1 6-ounce can tomato paste
  diluted in 1 cup water
6 whole allspice

Cut meat into 2-inch cubes and place in a Dutch oven. Add all remaining ingredients except the allspice. Cover tightly, bring to a boil, and simmer for 2 to 3 hours. Add the allspice, tied in cheese-cloth bag, during last hour of cooking, and continue to simmer until done. *6 servings*

BEEF POT ROAST *Vothino Entrada*

4 pounds pot roast
Salt and pepper
2 tablespoons flour
4 tablespoons butter
¼ cup red wine

3 onions, sliced
2 tablespoons tomato paste
2 cups water
1 bay leaf

Season the meat with salt and pepper and rub in the flour. Melt butter in Dutch oven and brown meat well on all sides. Add wine and sliced onions and sauté until onions wilt. Add tomato paste, dissolved in the water, and bay leaf. Cover and simmer for 3 hours. Serve with mashed potatoes or cooked rice. *8 servings*

Note: Diced carrots and celery may be added to this recipe.

OVEN BEEF STEW *Entrada tou Fournou*

3 pounds beef (top sirloin)
  cubed
3–4 carrots, quartered
6–8 small whole potatoes
3–4 celery stalks, halved

1 1-pound can Italian plum
  tomatoes
2 onions, chopped
Parsley, chopped
Salt and pepper

Place all ingredients in a roasting pan. Bake in a 350-degree oven for 2 hours, basting meat occasionally with sauce in pan. *6–8 servings*

PORK CHOPS WITH SAUERKRAUT
Païdakia Hirina me Lahano Toursi

6–8 pork chops, center cut
2 pounds sauerkraut
Tomato paste, paprika, or
   caraway seeds

2 cups water
Salt and pepper to taste

In skillet brown pork chops well. Put sauerkraut in a casserole. When chops are brown, drain drippings into sauerkraut. Add tomato paste, paprika, or caraway seeds. Place chops on top of sauerkraut and add water and salt and pepper. Cover and simmer for about 1 hour or until chops are very tender. This casserole may be baked in the oven if desired. *4–6 servings*

FRESH HAM MACARONADA   *Hirino Yahni Makaronada*

6 pounds fresh ham
4 tablespoons butter
Salt and pepper
Dash of cinnamon
3 onions, chopped
2 6-ounce cans tomato paste

2 quarts water
3 sticks cinnamon
1½ pounds macaroni
Browned butter
Grated cheese

Cut ham in 3-inch cubes. In skillet brown meat in half the butter; add salt and pepper and dash of cinnamon. In a large casserole brown onions in remaining butter until soft. Add meat, tomato paste, water, and cinnamon sticks. Simmer about 3 hours until sauce is thick and meat well done. Cook macaroni according to directions on package. Drain and empty into serving dish. Pour browned butter over macaroni; add grated cheese. Pour sauce and meat over all. Serve hot. *8–10 servings*

FRESH HAM WITH CELERY, AVGOLEMONO
Hirino Yahni me Selino Avgolemono

4–5-pounds fresh ham
4 tablespoons butter
2–3 onions, chopped
Water

Salt and pepper
2 bunches celery
AVGOLEMONO SAUCE

Cut ham in 2- or 3-inch cubes. Brown in butter with onions. Add water to cover and salt and pepper. Bring mixture to a boil, cover, and simmer until meat is almost done. Scrub and scrape celery and cut in 2-inch pieces. Add to meat and continue to simmer until meat and vegetable are done. Add *avgolemono* sauce according to directions. Serve warm. *8 servings*

LIVER IN CASSEROLE *Sikotaki Yahni*

1 pound lamb's liver	*Salt and pepper*
¼ cup red wine or wine vinegar	*2 tablespoons tomato paste*
3 onions, sliced	*(optional)*
¼ cup olive oil	*2 cups water*
Flour	*Oregano*

Cut liver into 1½-inch squares. Marinate meat in the wine or wine vinegar for 1 hour. In a casserole sauté onions in olive oil until lightly browned. Dredge meat with flour, add to onions, and brown. Add marinade and sprinkle with salt and pepper. Mix tomato paste and water and add to casserole. Sprinkle with oregano, cover, and simmer for 30 minutes. Serve with RICE PILAF. *4–6 servings*

GROUND MEAT DISHES

STUFFED VEGETABLES I *Yemista*

1½ pounds ground beef and lamb	*Green peppers*
	Zucchini
2 onions, chopped	*Salt*
Parsley, chopped	*Potatoes, sliced (optional)*
½ cup raw rice	*Onions, sliced (optional)*
Salt and pepper	*Butter*
Fresh or dried mint	*Olive oil*
Tomatoes	AVGOLEMONO SAUCE *(optional)*

Combine meat, chopped onions, parsley, rice, salt and pepper, and mint, and mix well, using enough water to moisten. Scoop out vegetables to be used for stuffing (tomatoes, green peppers, zucchini); save tomato pulp. Sprinkle salt inside and set vegetables aside. Add tomato pulp to meat mixture. Stuff vegetables and place in casserole or Dutch oven. Slices of potatoes and onions may be placed between vegetables. Dot with butter and sprinkle with olive oil. Add a little water. Cover and cook over low heat for 35 to 45 minutes or until vegetables are tender, basting occasionally. This may be served with thick *avgolemono* sauce. *6 servings*

STUFFED VEGETABLES II *Yemista*

2 onions, chopped	3¼ cups water
5 tablespoons butter	½ cup raw rice
1½ pounds ground beef	Green peppers
Salt and pepper	Tomatoes
Parsley and mint, chopped	Potatoes, sliced (optional)
3 tablespoons tomato paste	

Sauté onions in 3 tablespoons of the butter. Add beef and brown well. Season with salt and pepper and parsley and mint. Combine 1 tablespoon of the tomato paste with 1¼ cups of the water. Add rice and mix. Bring to a boil and cook until liquid is absorbed by rice. Mix rice with meat mixture. Cut thin slice from top of peppers and tomatoes, scoop out insides, and arrange vegetables in baking pan. Stuff with meat and rice mixture and cap with tops of vegetables. Dilute remaining tomato paste in remaining water and add to pan. Sliced potatoes may be placed between vegetables if desired. Dot with remaining butter. Bake in a 350-degree oven for about 1 hour or until vegetables are done, basting occasionally with the pan sauce. *6 servings*

STUFFED SQUASH *Kolokithakia Yemista*

1½ pounds ground beef	2 tablespoons tomato paste
2 onions, chopped	2 cups water
4 tablespoons butter	Grated cheese or cheese slices
Salt and pepper	AVGOLEMONO SAUCE (optional)
Dash of cinnamon	
2 pounds summer squash, split and scooped out	

Brown ground beef and onions in half the butter and add salt and pepper and cinnamon. Place squash in casserole and stuff. Dot with remaining butter. Add tomato paste mixed with water. Sprinkle with grated cheese or top with slices of cheese. Bake in a 350-degree oven for 1 hour. Stuffed squash may be served with *avgolemono* sauce, if desired; omit tomato paste if *avgolemono* sauce is served. *6 servings*

LITTLE SHOES *Papoutsakia*

6 medium eggplants	1 tablespoon parsley, chopped
½ cup butter	½ cup tomato sauce
1-2 onions, finely chopped	Grated cheese
½ pound ground lamb or beef	Parsley, chopped
Salt and pepper	1 cup boiling water

Cut eggplant in half lengthwise. Scoop out pulp and chop. Fry the shells in a little of the butter until they begin to soften and transfer to a baking dish. Add all but 2 tablespoons of the butter to butter remaining in skillet and in it sauté onions until golden. Add meat and continue to cook until meat is browned. Add eggplant pulp, salt and pepper, the 1 tablespoon chopped parsley, and tomato sauce. Mix well and simmer until most of the liquid is absorbed. Cool. Add grated cheese to taste and mix well.

Fill eggplant shells with the meat mixture and top each "little shoe" with additional grated cheese and chopped parsley. Dot with remaining butter. Add boiling water to pan and bake in a moderate 350-degree oven until eggplants are soft. Serve hot. *6 servings*

VARIATION: A cream sauce may be added to the top of the *papoutsakia* if desired. Use half the quantity of CREAM SAUCE recipe in sauce section. Stuff eggplant and spread a little of the sauce over the stuffing. Sprinkle with grated cheese. Add only ½ cup boiling water to pan instead of 1 cup, and the remaining butter. Cook in a 350-degree oven until sauce is browned and eggplant is tender.

STUFFED GRAPEVINE LEAVES WITH AVGOLEMONO SAUCE
Dolmadakia me Avgolemono

1½ pounds chopped meat	1 cup water
3 large onions, chopped	1 pound jar grapevine leaves
1 cup raw rice	3 bouillon cubes
Salt and pepper to taste	1 tablespoon butter
Dried mint leaves	

Combine meat, onions, rice, salt and pepper, and dried mint. Add water and mix well. Drain brine from jar of grapevine leaves, remove leaves, and wash well with clear water to remove all traces of brine. Put heaping tablespoon of meat and rice mixture in center of a leaf and roll leaf tightly, folding edges over and rolling toward point of leaf. Cover bottom of a greased Dutch oven or casserole with torn leaves. Arrange rolls in layers. Dissolve bouillon cubes in enough water to cover rolls, add the bouillon, and dot with butter. Cover with a heavy plate to keep rolls from opening as rice puffs, cover casserole, and steam over low heat for 1 hour. There should be some liquid left in casserole for gravy. If dry when cooking time is up, add water and simmer for a few minutes longer. *6–8 servings*

Avgolemono Sauce:
Beat 3 eggs well, add juice of 1 lemon, and beat well again. Add some of the hot gravy from the casserole, then pour egg mixture over the *dolmadakia*. Serve at once. If necessary to reheat, leave uncovered while warming very slowly, so egg sauce will not curdle.

MACEDONIAN STUFFED CABBAGE WITH THICK AVGOLEMONO *Sarmades me Avgolemono Pikto*

3–4 medium cabbages (outer leaves only)	*Salt and pepper to taste*
	2 onions, chopped
1 large can sauerkraut	*½ cup raw rice*
1½ pounds chopped beef	*2–3 lemons, peeled and sliced*
1½ pounds chopped pork	*Boiling water*

Fill a large pot with water and bring to a boil. Carefully remove outer leaves from cabbage heads, being careful not to tear them, and parboil about 5 minutes. Drain in a colander. Place sauerkraut in bottom of Dutch oven. Cover with a few cabbage leaves. Thoroughly combine beef, pork, salt and pepper, chopped onions, and rice. Carefully remove heavy center vein from remaining cabbage leaves and cut each leaf in 2. Place 1 rounded tablespoon of meat mixture near cut end of leaf; fold over. Fold edges in toward center and roll up tightly. Place rolls in casserole with lemon slices between the layers. Cover with an inverted heavy plate to act as weight. Add enough boiling water to cover rim of plate. Cover casserole, bring slowly to a boil, and simmer gently for 3 hours.

Thick Avgolemono Sauce:

4 eggs
1 lemon, juice of
2 cups hot broth

Beat eggs well, adding juice of lemon. Gradually add hot broth, beating constantly. Cook over low heat, stirring constantly, until sauce thickens. *8 servings*

STUFFED CABBAGE LEAVES *Lahanodolmades*

2 medium cabbages (outer leaves only)
1 pound ground meat
2 onions, chopped
3 tablespoons butter
Salt and pepper

2 tablespoons tomato paste
Cinnamon
1 cup boiling water
¼ cup raw rice
Boiling water
Lemon slices

Parboil cabbage leaves as in recipe above. Brown ground beef and chopped onions in 2 tablespoons of the butter. Add salt and pepper, half the tomato paste, and cinnamon. Add water and rice. Simmer until rice is partially done. Stuff cabbage leaves as described in recipe above. Cover bottom of a greased casserole with cabbage leaves. Place rolls in layers. Cover with inverted plate. Add remaining tomato paste diluted with enough boiling water to cover rim of plate. Dot with remaining butter. Cover and simmer for 2 hours or until done. Serve with lemon slices. *6 servings*

STUFFED CABBAGE LEAVES WITH PORK *Sarmades*

1½ pounds chopped pork
2 onions, chopped
¼ cup olive oil
½ cup raw rice

Dried mint
Salt and pepper
2–3 cabbages
AVGOLEMONO SAUCE

Sauté pork and onions in oil until browned. Add rice, mint, and salt and pepper. Parboil large cabbage leaves and roll meat mixture in leaves according to recipe for MACEDONIAN STUFFED CABBAGE. Place in greased casserole. Cover with water and large cabbage leaf. Weigh down with inverted plate. Cover casserole and cook over low heat for 2 to 3 hours or until done. Serve with *avgolemono* sauce. *6 servings*

MOUSSAKA I

4 medium eggplants
Salt
4 tablespoons butter
2 pounds ground beef
3 onions, chopped
2 tablespoons tomato paste
¼ cup parsley, chopped
½ cup red wine
Salt and pepper
½ cup water
Dash cinnamon

2–3 eggs, beaten
½ cup grated cheese
½ cup bread crumbs
6 tablespoons butter
6 tablespoons flour
3 cups hot milk
Salt and pepper to taste
Dash nutmeg
4 egg yolks, lightly beaten
Cooking oil
Grated cheese

Remove ½-inch-wide strips of peel lengthwise from eggplants, leaving ½-inch peel between the strips. Cut into thick slices, sprinkle with salt, and let stand between two heavy plates while browning meat and making sauce.

In frying pan melt the 4 tablespoons butter and in it sauté meat and onions until meat is browned. Add tomato paste, parsley, wine, salt and pepper, and water. Simmer until liquid is absorbed. Cool. Stir in cinnamon, eggs, cheese, and half the bread crumbs.

Make sauce: In saucepan melt the 6 tablespoons butter over low heat. Add flour and stir until well blended. Remove from heat. Gradually stir in milk. Return to heat and cook, stirring, until sauce is thick and smooth. Add salt and pepper to taste and the nutmeg. Combine egg yolks with a little of the hot sauce, then stir egg mixture into sauce and cook over very low heat for 2 minutes, stirring constantly.

Brown eggplant slices on both sides in hot oil. Grease an ovenproof casserole and sprinkle bottom with remaining bread crumbs. Cover with layer of eggplant slices, then a layer of meat, and continue until all eggplant and meat is used, finishing with a layer of eggplant. Cover with sauce, sprinkle with grated cheese, and bake in a 350-degree oven for 1 hour. Serve hot. *10–12 servings*

MOUSSAKA II

2 large onions, chopped	5–6 eggplants
½ pound butter	Salt
4 pounds ground beef	6 eggs
Salt and pepper to taste	4 cups milk
Oregano	½ cup flour
Dash garlic powder	1 teaspoon salt
1 2-pound 3-ounce can Italian plum tomatoes	2 tablespoons butter
	Grated cheese
1 cup tomato purée or sauce	

Brown onions in ¼ pound of the butter. Add ground beef and brown well. Add salt and pepper, oregano, and garlic powder. Add tomatoes and tomato purée or sauce and cook over low heat for 1 hour, stirring frequently. Set aside.

Melt remaining ¼ pound butter. Peel one eggplant at a time. Cut lengthwise into ½-inch-thick slices and arrange slices on broiler pan. Sprinkle lightly with salt and brush with melted butter. Brown 2 inches from broiler heat, turn, and brown other side. Set aside and repeat until all eggplants are peeled and broiled.

Beat eggs with 1 cup of the milk, the flour, and teaspoon salt. Heat remaining milk with the 2 tablespoons butter. Add slowly to egg mixture, beating constantly. Stir over low heat, without letting sauce boil, until very thick.

Overlap a layer of eggplant in bottom of an ungreased 10×16×2-inch pan and sprinkle lightly with grated cheese. Cover eggplant with meat mixture and sprinkle again with cheese. Repeat layers until all eggplant and meat is used, ending with a layer of eggplant. Cover top with the egg sauce and sprinkle generously with grated cheese. Bake in a 375-degree oven for about 1 hour or until golden brown. Cut into squares and serve warm.

Note: Eggplant and meat may be prepared in the casserole a day before using and stored in refrigerator. Next day, prepare egg sauce and bake. *14–16 servings*

MOUSSAKA III

2 *medium eggplants*	*¼ cup bread crumbs*
Salt	*4 small zucchini, sliced*
Olive oil	*4 medium potatoes, thinly*
1½ pounds ground beef	*sliced*
2 onions, chopped	*Grated cheese*
¾ cup butter	*½ cup water*
1 teaspoon tomato paste	*¾ cup flour*
Dash cinnamon	*1 quart hot milk*
Salt and pepper to taste	*6 eggs*

Slice eggplant, sprinkle with salt, and place in a colander. Weigh down with a heavy plate for several hours. Then brush slices with oil and broil lightly. Sauté beef and onions in 5 tablespoons of the butter. Add tomato paste, cinnamon, and salt and pepper and mix well. Sprinkle bottom of a greased baking dish with bread crumbs. Alternate layers of vegetables and meat in the pan, sprinkling each layer with cheese. The top layer should be vegetables. Dot with 1 tablespoon butter and add water. Set aside.

In saucepan melt remaining 6 tablespoons butter. Add flour and cook, stirring, until well mixed and beginning to brown. Slowly stir in milk and cook, stirring, until sauce is smooth and thickened. Beat eggs with a little of the hot sauce, then stir into remaining sauce. Remove from heat. Pour a little more than half the sauce over the vegetables and bake in a 350-degree oven for 10 minutes. Meanwhile return remaining sauce to low heat and cook, stirring, until thick. Pour into casserole and sprinkle with cheese. Continue to bake for 45 to 50 minutes longer or until golden brown. *8 servings*

PASTICHIO I

For this famous Greek dish you need to make two cream sauces, one thin and one heavy, as follows:

Thin Cream Sauce:

4 tablespoons butter	*2 cups hot milk*
⅓ cup flour	*2 egg yolks*

Melt butter in a saucepan. Stir in flour and cook until mixture turns golden. Gradually stir in hot milk and cook, stirring, until sauce is smooth and hot. Beat egg yolks with a little of the hot milk and stir into sauce. Remove from heat without cooking the eggs.

Thick Cream Sauce:

2 cups milk	½ cup flour
4 eggs	2 cups cold milk

Heat 2 cups milk to simmering. Beat eggs with flour. Stir in cold milk. Gradually stir in the hot milk and cook, stirring constantly, until mixture is quite thick. Do not let boil after eggs are added.

3 onions, chopped	Garlic powder
1½ pounds chopped beef	½ cup bread crumbs
4 tablespoons butter	2 egg whites
2 cups Italian plum tomatoes	1¼ pounds macaroni, ziti #2
1 cup tomato sauce	Thin cream sauce
Oregano	Grated cheese
Dash cinnamon	Thick cream sauce
Salt and pepper to taste	

Brown chopped onions and meat in butter. Add tomatoes, tomato sauce, spices, and seasonings. Cover and simmer for 1 hour. Cool and stir in part of bread crumbs and the egg whites, unbeaten.

Cook macaroni according to directions on package and drain.

Sprinkle remaining bread crumbs into a buttered 11×16×2-inch baking pan. Put in a layer of macaroni, a layer of meat with sauce, and half the thin cream sauce. Sprinkle with grated cheese. Add another layer of macaroni and sprinkle with cheese. Cover with remaining thin cream sauce. Spread the thick cream sauce over top and sprinkle with cheese. Bake in a 350-degree oven for 1 hour. Cool and slice into squares. When ready to serve, reheat in hot oven.

Note: This dish may be prepared a day in advance. Do not top with the thick cream sauce, but add it just before baking the dish. *12 servings*

PASTICHIO II

Cream Sauce:

1 quart milk	¾ cup cold water
½ pound butter	12 eggs
⅓ cup cornstarch	

Heat milk and butter to boiling point. Combine cornstarch and water and stir into hot milk mixture. Cook, stirring, until sauce thickens. Cool a little. Beat 12 eggs and gradually beat in the hot sauce. Set aside.

1 onion, chopped
¼ cup butter
½ cup water
2 pounds ground lamb or beef
4 cloves garlic, chopped
3 ounces (½ can) tomato paste

1 teaspoon cinnamon
Salt and pepper to taste
1 pound macaroni, ziti #2
½ pound Romano cheese, grated
Cream sauce

Sauté onion in butter until golden. Add water, cover, and simmer until onion is soft. Add meat, garlic, tomato paste, cinnamon, and salt and pepper and cook, stirring, until meat is browned.

Cook macaroni according to directions on package. Drain.

Arrange layers of macaroni and meat sauce in a greased baking dish, sprinkling each layer with cheese. Cover with about half the cream sauce and bake in a 400-degree oven for 5 minutes. Add remaining cream sauce, sprinkle with cheese, and bake for 5 minutes longer. Reduce oven temperature to 325 degrees and bake for 40 to 50 minutes or until nicely browned and set. *12 servings*

PASTICHIO III (Simplified)

Cream Sauce:

6 tablespoons butter
¾ cup flour
1 quart hot milk

2 teaspoons salt
3 eggs

Melt butter in a saucepan. Add flour and cook, stirring, until mixture is golden. Gradually stir in hot milk. Cook, stirring constantly, until sauce is smooth and thickened. Stir in salt and set aside to cool. When partly cool stir in eggs, lightly beaten.

2 onions, chopped
4 tablespoons butter
2 pounds ground meat
Dash of cinnamon
Salt and pepper
½ cup water

2 tablespoons tomato paste
1 pound elbow macaroni
3 eggs, beaten
1 tablespoon salt
Grated cheese
Cream sauce

Sauté onions in butter until golden. Add meat and cook, stirring, until meat is browned. Add cinnamon and salt and pepper to taste. Add water and tomato paste and cook for 5 minutes.

Cook macaroni according to directions on package. Drain and rinse. When lukewarm add eggs and the 1 tablespoon salt to the macaroni and mix well.

Put half the macaroni in a buttered 9×13×2-inch pan and sprinkle generously with grated cheese. Add meat mixture and sprinkle with cheese. Add remaining macaroni and sprinkle with cheese. Bake in a 350-degree oven for 10 minutes. Top with cream sauce, sprinkle with cheese, and bake for 30 minutes longer or until well browned. *8–10 servings*

MEAT TARTS *Kreatopetes*

Pastry Dough:

2 cups flour	⅓ cup shortening
2½ teaspoons baking powder	¾ cup milk
1 teaspoon salt	

In mixing bowl combine flour, baking powder, and salt. Cut in shortening with pastry blender or 2 knives. Stir in about ¾ cup milk, or enough to make a dough that is soft but not sticky. Set aside.

½ pound ground beef	Salt and pepper to taste
2 small onions, chopped	2 hard-cooked eggs, finely
2 tablespoons butter	chopped
2 tomatoes, peeled and thinly sliced	Pastry dough
1 tablespoon parsley or dill, minced	Milk or beaten egg

Sauté meat and onions in butter until lightly browned. Add tomatoes, parsley or dill, and salt and pepper to taste and simmer a few minutes. Don't let tomatoes get too soft. Remove from heat and stir in eggs.

Roll out dough thinly on lightly floured board and cut into squares. Put a spoonful of meat mixture on each square and fold over into triangles. Moisten edges with water and seal. Brush with milk or beaten egg. Bake at 400 degrees for 30 minutes. If desired, serve with garlic-flavored yogurt sauce. *6–8 servings*

MANTI

Pastry Dough:

2 cups flour	2 tablespoons oil
1 teaspoon salt	¾ cup water

Combine flour and salt. Work in oil and about ¾ cup water. Knead dough lightly. If it seems too stiff add a little more oil and water without making dough sticky. Set aside to rest.

1 onion, chopped	2 cups water
2 pounds ground meat	2 cups TRAHANA (noodles)
3 tablespoons butter	Pastry dough
Salt to taste	4 cups hot chicken broth

Sauté onion and meat in butter until lightly browned. Add salt. Add water and bring to a boil. Add *trahana* and cook for 10 minutes, or until most of the liquid is absorbed. Cool.

Roll out dough thinly on lightly floured board. Cut one piece large enough to fit a 10×14-inch pan. Cut rest of dough into squares. Place a spoonful of filling in center of each square and bring corners together. Moisten edges, seal, and twist the little triangles. Arrange the "twists" in the buttered pan and cover with the large piece of pastry. Prick pastry. Bake in a 350-degree oven for 45 minutes, or until pastry is golden. Remove from oven and pour the hot chicken broth over the *manti*. Let stand until most of the broth is absorbed. *8 servings*

ZUCCHINI SOUFFLE   *Sfogato*

1 pound ground lamb	2 teaspoons parsley, chopped
3 onions, finely chopped	1 teaspoon salt
4 tablespoons butter	1 cup water
1 pound small zucchini, cubed	8 eggs
Dash pepper	TOMATO SAUCE

Sauté lamb and onions in butter until meat is browned. Add zucchini, pepper, parsley, salt, and water and cook over low heat, stirring occasionally, until meat and vegetables are tender. Cool slightly. Beat eggs until frothy. Stir into cooked mixture. Pour into a 1-quart baking dish or soufflé dish and bake in a 375-degree oven for 30 minutes or until set. Cut into squares and serve hot with tomato sauce. *6 servings*

KEFTAIDES

See recipe for KEFTAIDAKIA (COCKTAIL MEATBALLS). For family meals, shape the meat into 2-inch balls instead of cocktail size. Wine may be omitted and garlic added to taste.

MEATBALLS A LA SMYRNA *Smyrnaika Souzoukakia*

Tomato Sauce:

1 2-pound 3-ounce can peeled tomatoes, mashed	1 clove garlic, minced (optional)
1 6-ounce can tomato paste	1 bay leaf
	Salt and pepper to taste

In saucepan combine tomatoes, tomato paste, garlic, if desired, bay leaf, and salt and pepper. Bring to a boil and simmer for 1 hour.

1 pound ground meat	1 clove garlic, minced
2 slices bread, crumbed	Dash cinnamon
1 teaspoon salt	¼ pound butter
½ teaspoon pepper or to taste	Tomato sauce
½ teaspoon kimino* (cumin seed)	

Combine meat, bread, salt, pepper, cumin, garlic, and cinnamon. Shape into small sausages and brown in butter. When cooked drop into tomato sauce and add any butter and dripping left in the pan in which the meatballs were browned. *4–6 servings*

Note: The tomato sauce is excellent served over rice, manestra,* macaroni, or mashed potatoes. Serve with a side dish of grated cheese.

GREEK MEAT SAUCE FOR MACARONI *Makaronada*

2 onions, chopped	Pepper
1 clove garlic, finely chopped	1 6-ounce can tomato paste
3 tablespoons butter	2 cups water
1 pound ground beef	Dash of cinnamon
1½ teaspoons salt	Dash of ground cloves

Sauté onions and garlic in butter. Add meat and brown, seasoning with salt and pepper. Blend tomato paste and water, add to mixture, and bring to a boil. Add spices and simmer for 1 hour. Serve over macaroni. Serve with grated cheese. *4–6 servings*

PASA MAKAROUNA

Noodle Dough:

> 8 cups flour, sifted
> 1 teaspoon salt
> 6–8 eggs

In a large bowl combine flour and salt. Make a well in center and add eggs, one at a time, working each one in with hands to make a firm dough that is smooth enough to be rolled out. It must not be sticky, so it may not be necessary to add the last egg. Cover with towel to prevent dough from drying out and set aside.

> 2 pounds ground round steak
> 4–6 tablespoons butter
> Salt and pepper to taste
> Noodle dough
> Boiling salted water
>
> Cold water
> ½ pound Kefalotiri,* grated
> 1 quart hot chicken or beef
>   broth

Sauté meat in butter until browned. Season with salt and pepper and set aside.

Roll out portions of the dough very thinly on a lightly floured board and cut each portion into a rectangle 12×15×2 inches. Sprinkle each sheet of dough with flour and keep covered with a towel to prevent drying.

Line a greased baking pan, 12×15 inches, with a sheet of the noodle dough. Set aside another sheet for the top of the pie. The top and bottom sheets of the *pasta* are not cooked, but the remaining sheets are cooked as follows: Have ready a large pot of boiling salted water and one of cold water. Carefully take one layer of dough at a time and toss into the boiling water. Boil for 2 to 3 minutes. Remove and plunge into cold water. Remove and squeeze out excess moisture.

Cover the uncooked layer of dough in the pan with ground meat and sprinkle with grated cheese. Add each additional layer of cooked dough as it is ready. Cover with layer of meat and sprinkle with cheese. Continue until all layers of dough have been cooked and added to the pan. Cover with the last, uncooked, layer of dough and score this in squares with a sharp knife. Bake in a 300-degree oven for 1 hour. After 30 minutes' baking time, slowly add the hot broth. If the top crust gets too brown before cooking time is finished, cover with aluminum foil. Serve warm. *8 servings*

VEGETABLES & SALADS

VINEGAR

VEGETABLES AND SALADS

On the rocky, arid terrain of Greece, the olive tree flourishes and provides Greece not only with a thriving industry, but with a food product that is the basis of her cuisine.

The olive tree is as old as the mythological history of Greece. The Greek goddess Athene, who bequeathed her name to the capital city of Athens, caused the olive tree to be born and, when she and Poseidon, who had opened a salt spring with his trident in the rock on which the Acropolis was later built, fought for supremacy over the Atheneans, the gods decided in favor of Athene because in their estimation the olive was a greater gift to mankind than salt.

Since ancient times the olive has been a symbol of peace and victorious warriors were crowned with the leafy branches of the olive tree. From the wood of the tree the arrows of Herakles, the scepters of kings, and the crooks of shepherds were made.

In Greek cooking vegetables are simmered until tender in olive oil, and olive oil is used as a dressing on both vegetables and salad greens. It is combined with either lemon, vinegar, or tomatoes, but it is interesting to note that in Greek cooking lemon and tomatoes, are used interchangeably with olive oil, but never at the same time.

The Greeks are partial to vegetables, especially eggplant, artichokes, and cabbage, and often make a complete meal of them. And salad is indispensable on every table. The Greek philosopher Aristoxenus is said to have loved lettuce so much that he watered his lettuce garden with the sweet wine of Chios.

In addition to the usual salad greens such as lettuce, romaine, and escarole, the Greeks appreciate the more pungent flavors of wild chickory and dandelion greens in their salads. Herbs, too, are popular, and the aromatic flavors of dill, mint, and oregano are used to flavor both vegetables and salads.

VEGETABLES

ARTICHOKES A LA POLITIKA *Anginares à la Polita*

6 *artichokes*
3 *lemons*
4 *tablespoons flour*
½ *cup finely chopped onion*
1½ *cups olive oil*

12 *small whole onions*
Water
Salt
Pinch of sugar
½ *bunch dill, finely chopped*

Prepare artichokes by breaking off outer 3 layers of leaves. Slice off 1 inch of the tips and a small portion of stem. Scrape upper portion and stem of artichoke to remove the outer dark green, and remove the purple choke with a spoon. Rub artichokes with a cut lemon and drop into a bowl of cold water into which has been mixed the juice of 1 lemon and the flour.

Simmer chopped onion in ½ cup of the olive oil until soft. Add whole white onions, water to cover, the juice of 1 lemon, remaining olive oil, salt, and sugar. Bring mixture to a boil and add prepared artichokes and chopped dill. Cook slowly for 30 minutes. Allow to cool in the sauce and serve cold. *6 servings*

ARTICHOKES WITH BUTTER SAUCE *Anginares Voutiro*

10 *small artichokes*
4 *lemons*
4 *tablespoons flour plus 1*
  teaspoon
½ *cup butter*

2–3 *onions, finely chopped*
Water
Salt and pepper
¼ *cup dill, finely chopped*

Prepare artichokes by breaking off the 3 outer layers of leaves at the breaking point. Slice off 1 inch of the tips and a small portion of the stem. Slice in half and remove the purple choke. Scrape upper portion and stem to remove the dark green. Rub all cut surfaces with a cut lemon as you work and drop into a bowl of cold water into which has been mixed the juice of 1 lemon and the 4 tablespoons flour.

In a large casserole melt butter and in it sauté the onion until golden and soft. Stir in the 1 teaspoon flour. Add enough water to cover the artichokes, salt and pepper, dill, and the juice of 2 lemons.

Bring to a boil, drain the artichokes, and add them to casserole. Cover and simmer for about 45 minutes or until artichokes are tender. Remove artichokes to a platter and keep warm. Bring the liquid to a rapid boil and cook until reduced and thickened to sauce consistency. Pour over artichokes and serve. *5 servings*

FRIED ARTICHOKES *Anginares Tighanites*

6–8 artichokes	2 eggs
2 lemons	1 tablespoon warm water
4 tablespoons flour	½ cup bread crumbs
Boiling water	
Fat for deep frying (preferably a mixture of olive oil and vegetable oil)	

Prepare artichokes as in recipe for ARTICHOKES WITH BUTTER SAUCE, using lemon juice and flour. Place halved artichokes in a kettle and cover with boiling water. Cover and simmer for 30 to 45 minutes or until tender. Drain thoroughly. Beat eggs until light with the 1 tablespoon warm water. Dip artichoke halves in egg, then in bread crumbs, and again in egg. Fry in hot deep fat until golden brown. *3–4 servings*

ARTICHOKES WITH FAVA BEANS *Anginares me Koukia*

2 onions or bunch of scallions, chopped	Salt and pepper
¼ cup butter	1 lemon, juice of
1 tablespoon flour	1 pound fava beans,* cleaned
Water	1 package frozen artichoke hearts
Dill	½ cup milk
Parsley, chopped	1 egg

Brown chopped onions or scallions lightly in butter. Stir in flour and about ½ cup water. Add dill, parsley, and salt and pepper. Add juice of ½ lemon, fava beans, and water to cover. Bring to a boil, cover, and simmer for 20 minutes. Add artichoke hearts and continue cooking until vegetables are tender. When cooked, strain juice and add milk. Beat egg with remaining lemon juice and gradually beat in the hot milk mixture. Cook over low heat, stirring constantly, until sauce coats the spoon. Pour over vegetables and serve warm. *4–6 servings*

BOILED VEGETABLES *Horta Vrasta*

Chicory   *Kale*
Dandelion greens   *Spinach*
Endive   *String beans*
Escarole   *Squash*

Any of the above vegetables may be boiled in salted water until tender and served as a salad with lemon juice and olive oil. These may be served hot or cold. Chopped parsley may be added as a garnish on the squash.

BRAISED CHICK-PEAS *Revithia Yahni*

2 pounds chick-peas
3 quarts water
1–2 cloves garlic, crushed
3–4 onions, finely chopped

2 cups peeled, chopped tomatoes, drained
½ cup parsley or mint, chopped
Salt and freshly ground black pepper

Soak chick-peas in water overnight. Drain and transfer to a heavy kettle or Dutch oven. Add water, bring to a boil, and simmer for 4 hours. When soft add garlic, onion, tomatoes, parsley or mint, and salt and pepper. Simmer over low heat for 20 minutes longer. *6–8 servings*

CHICK-PEAS WITH RICE PILAF *Revithia me Pilafi*

1 1-pound 4-ounce can chick-peas
1 onion, finely chopped
4 tablespoons olive oil

Salt and pepper to taste
1 lemon, juice of
RICE PILAF

Drain chick-peas, reserving ½ cup of the liquid. Sauté onion in olive oil until golden. Add chick-peas and continue to cook for about 5 minutes. Add reserved chick-pea liquid, salt and pepper, and lemon juice. Bring to a boil and simmer for 10 minutes. Serve over rice *pilaf*. *4 servings*

BRAISED EGGPLANT *Melitzanes Plaki*

2–3 medium eggplants
Salt and pepper
Olive oil or olive oil and
    vegetable oil combined
1 onion, sliced

½ cup parsley, chopped
3–4 tomatoes, thinly sliced
1–2 cloves garlic, slivered
1 bay leaf

Slice eggplant, sprinkle with salt and pepper, and put in a colander to drain. Weigh down with a heavy plate and let stand for 30 minutes. Heat oil in a skillet and quickly brown eggplant slices on both sides, adding more oil as needed. When all slices have been browned, there should be 2 to 3 tablespoons oil remaining in the skillet. In this oil sauté onion until soft and golden. Return eggplant slices and add parsley, tomatoes, garlic, and bay leaf. Cook over low heat for 45 minutes. *4–6 servings*

FRIED EGGPLANT *Melitzana Tighaniti*

1–2 large eggplants
Salt

Olive oil for frying, or half olive
    oil and half shortening
SKORDALIA SAUCE

Remove ½-inch-lengthwise strips of peel from eggplants, leaving ½-inch strips of peel between. Cut eggplant into thick slices, sprinkle with salt and place in a colander to drain. Weigh down with a heavy plate and let stand for 30 minutes. In a large skillet heat the oil and in it brown eggplant on both sides, adding more oil as necessary. Serve with *skordalia* sauce. *6–8 servings*

IMAM BAILDI

1 large eggplant
Salt
1 cup olive oil
1 pound onions, sliced
3 large tomatoes, peeled and
    chopped

3 cloves garlic, minced
Parsley, chopped
Salt and pepper
½ cup water

Remove leaves from stem end of eggplant. Pare lengthwise in 1-inch strips, leaving 1-inch strips of skin between. Make incisions in the pared portions, sprinkle eggplant with salt, and allow to stand for about 10 minutes.

In a heavy kettle brown eggplant in ½ cup of the olive oil for 5 minutes, turning 2 or 3 times. Combine remaining oil, onions, tomatoes, garlic, and parsley. Stuff this mixture into incisions in eggplant. Return eggplant to kettle and add water and any remaining vegetable mixture. Bring to a boil, cover, and simmer for 40 minutes or until done. Cool before serving and serve cold. *4–6 servings*

BRAISED ENDIVE, AVGOLEMONO *Andithia Avgolemono*

4 large heads Belgian endive, halved	1 tablespoon lemon juice
Ice water	1 cup meat or chicken stock
¼ cup butter	2 eggs
Salt and pepper	1 lemon, juice of

Soak endive in ice water for 15 minutes to crisp. Dry carefully with paper towels. In a skillet melt butter and in it arrange the endive. Add salt and pepper and the 1 tablespoon lemon juice and brown the endive lightly for 2 minutes on each side. Add the stock, ¼ cup at a time, and simmer the endive, uncovered, for 25 to 30 minutes or until tender. Beat eggs with lemon juice. Slowly beat in the broth from the skillet. Pour the *avgolemono* sauce over the endive and serve immediately. *4–6 servings*

FAVA

1 cup yellow split peas	1 teaspoon salt
1 onion, finely chopped	¼ teaspoon oregano
1 clove garlic, finely chopped	Parsley, minced
3 tablespoons butter	Olive oil

Wash peas, cover with water, and bring to a boil. Remove scum. Sauté onion and garlic in butter until golden. Add to peas with salt and oregano. Simmer, covered, until water is absorbed. Stir occasionally with a wooden spoon. Before serving, sprinkle with parsley and olive oil. Serve hot or cold. *4–6 servings*

BRAISED FAVA BEANS *Koukia Yahni*

4 onions, finely chopped
¾ cup olive oil
6 tomatoes, thinly sliced
¼ cup parsley, chopped
Salt and pepper to taste

2 cups water
3 pounds fresh fava beans* or
   3 packages frozen fava beans,
   defrosted

Sauté onions in olive oil until golden. Add tomatoes, parsley, salt and pepper, and water. Bring to a boil. Add fava beans and weigh them down with a heavy plate. Cover casserole and simmer for about 35 minutes or until beans are cooked. *6 servings*

BRAISED OKRA *Bamyes Yahni*

1 pound fresh or frozen okra
½ cup vinegar
2–3 small onions, finely
   chopped
½ cup olive oil

1½ cups canned tomatoes
1 tablespoon parsley, chopped
Salt and pepper to taste
Water to cover
2–3 lemon slices (optional)

Wash fresh okra and trim by removing cone-shaped portions at top. Place okra in bowl, sprinkle with vinegar, and allow to stand for 1 to 2 hours. Rinse thoroughly in cold water. Sauté onions in part of the olive oil. When browned, add tomatoes gradually. Cook for 2 minutes, then add okra, parsley, salt and pepper, remaining olive oil, and sufficient water to cover. Add lemon slices if desired. Bring to a boil, lower heat, and cook for 30 minutes or until okra is tender. *4–6 servings*

BRAISED POTATOES *Patates Yahni*

2–3 onions, finely chopped
½ cup olive oil
6–8 medium potatoes, peeled
   and sliced

2 tablespoons tomato paste
Salt and pepper
Water to cover

Sauté onions in olive oil until golden brown. Add potatoes, tomato paste, salt and pepper, and enough water to cover. Cover casserole, bring liquid to a boil, and simmer for about 30 minutes or until potatoes are cooked. Cool a little before serving. *6 servings*

SPINACH AND RICE *Spanakorizo*

2 large onions, finely chopped
¾ cup olive oil
1 teaspoon tomato paste
1 pound spinach or 2 packages
    frozen spinach

About 1 cup water
Salt and pepper
2 sprigs fresh mint (optional)
½ cup raw rice

Sauté onions in oil until soft. Add tomato paste and spinach and stir. Add water to cover and bring to a boil. Add seasonings. Sprinkle rice on top. Do not stir. Cover and simmer until rice is cooked. *4–6 servings*

VARIATION: To above ingredients add 3 tomatoes, sliced. Sauté onion in oil, add tomatoes, and simmer until sauce is thickened. Add spinach, 1 cup rice, mint, and water as needed. Cover and simmer until rice is cooked.

FRIED SQUASH *Kolokethia Tighanita*

3–4 onions, finely chopped
½ cup olive oil or butter
1 tablespoon tomato paste
3–4 tablespoons parsley,
    chopped

Salt and pepper
Water
3 pounds summer squash

Sauté onion in olive oil or butter until soft and golden. Add tomato paste, parsley, salt and pepper, and water to a depth of 2 inches. Bring to a boil. Scrape or peel the squash and cut into chunks. Add to casserole, cover, and simmer for about 20 minutes or until squash is tender and sauce is slightly thickened. *6 servings*

FRIED SQUASH *Kolokethia Tiganita*

Cut squash into 1-inch-thick slices. Season with salt and pepper and dust with flour. Fry in hot olive oil or a combination of olive oil and vegetable oil until golden brown on both sides. Serve with SKORDALIA SAUCE.

SQUASH FRITTERS *Kolokethokeftaides*

1½ pounds summer squash	3–4 cups bread crumbs
Boiling salted water	2 tablespoons butter, melted
1 large onion, finely chopped	2 eggs
Salt and pepper	Flour
3 tablespoons grated cheese	Olive oil and butter for frying

Peel squash, cut in half, and cook in boiling salted water, with the onion, until soft. Drain thoroughly and mash until smooth. Add salt and pepper, cheese, bread crumbs, melted butter, and eggs and mix well. Let stand for 1 hour. Then shape into 1½-inch balls, roll in flour, and fry in part olive oil and part butter until golden on all sides. *4 servings*

VARIATION: An additional finely chopped onion, sautéed in butter, may be added to the mashed squash with the other ingredients if desired.

BAKED ZUCCHINI I *Kolokithopeta*

4 to 5 zucchini, scraped	¾ cup olive oil
1 medium onion or 1 bunch scallions, sliced	1 cup water
	1 tablespoon flour
1 cup parsley, chopped	Paprika or sliced tomatoes for garnish
Salt and pepper to taste	

Slice the zucchini lengthwise ¼ inch thick. Arrange the slices in a baking dish in layers alternately with the onions. Sprinkle with parsley and salt and pepper to taste. Pour olive oil and water over all and sprinkle with flour. Bake in a 350-degree oven for about 40 minutes or until zucchini is tender. Just before serving sprinkle with paprika or garnish with sliced tomatoes. *4–6 servings*

BAKED ZUCCHINI II *Kolokithia Psita*

2 pounds zucchini	Parmesan or Romano cheese, grated
2 tablespoons tomato paste	
2 cups water	Grated sharp cheddar
¼ cup olive oil	Oregano

Scrape zucchini and slice in half lengthwise. Arrange zucchini in a baking pan, cut side up. Combine tomato paste, water, and olive oil and pour over the zucchini. Sprinkle with Parmesan or Romano and cheddar cheese. Sprinkle with oregano and bake in a 375-degree oven for 30 minutes or until zucchini is tender. *4–6 servings*

BRAISED STRING BEANS *Fassoulakia Yahni*

1 large onion, chopped
1 small clove garlic, minced
  (optional)
¾ cup olive oil
1 teaspoon tomato paste

½ fresh tomato, peeled and
  chopped
1 pound string beans
Parsley or fresh mint, chopped
Salt and pepper
Water

Sauté onion and garlic in olive oil until soft. Add tomato paste and fresh tomato and simmer until sauce is slightly thickened. Add string beans and seasoning and enough water to cover. Cover and cook until beans are tender. *4–6 servings*

STUFFED TOMATOES LADERES *Yemistes Domates Laderes*

12 tomatoes
Salt
Pinch of sugar
3 onions, grated
1½ cups olive oil
⅓ cup parsley, chopped

½ cup dill, chopped
½ cup raisins or currants
½ cup pignolia nuts
1 cup rice
Salt and pepper
½ cup water

Wash tomatoes and scoop out pulp; save caps. Sprinkle inside of tomatoes with salt and sugar. Sauté onions in ¼ cup of the olive oil until soft. Mix onions, parsley, dill, raisins or currants, pignolia nuts, rice, and 1 cup of the olive oil. Season to taste with salt and pepper. Fill tomatoes with this mixture. Cover with tomato caps and place in casserole with remaining ¼ cup olive oil and the water. Weigh down tomatoes with a heavy plate. Cover casserole and simmer for about 30 minutes or until rice is done. Serve cold. *12 servings*

TOMATOES STUFFED WITH RICE *Yemistes Domates me Rizi*

6 ripe but firm tomatoes	6 tablespoons raw rice
1 bunch Italian parsley, chopped	4 tablespoons olive oil
¼ cup mint, chopped	1 cup tomato sauce
¼ head garlic, chopped	Parmesan or Romano cheese, grated
2 large onions, chopped	3 teaspoons olive oil
2 tablespoons butter	1 cup water

Wash tomatoes. Partially cut through a slice at top, but without detaching it, and scoop out tomato pulp. Discard seeds and chop pulp. Mix pulp with parsley, mint, and garlic. Sauté onions in butter until golden. Add tomato mixture and cook, stirring, for a few minutes. Stir in rice, the 4 tablespoons olive oil, and ¼ cup of the tomato sauce. Simmer for 5 minutes. If the mixture is too thick, add a little water. It is important that the mixture be not too juicy, but have enough liquid so the rice can cook. Fill tomatoes ¾ full of the mixture. Sprinkle with cheese and add ½ teaspoon olive oil to each tomato. Cover with partially removed slice. Arrange tomatoes in a baking pan. Add the water mixed with remaining tomato sauce and bake in a 350-degree oven for 45 minutes to 1 hour, basting occasionally with liquid in pan. *6 servings*

VARIATION: Add diced, cooked shrimp to rice mixture.

BULGUR *Pligouri*

1½ cups rich stock	1 cup bulgur*
Salt and pepper	Butter

Bring stock to a boil. Add salt to taste and the *bulgur*. Cover and cook over low heat for about 25 minutes or until *bulgur* is cooked. Correct seasoning and add butter. The amount of butter depends on the richness of the stock. *4 servings*

RICE PILAF I *Rizi Pilafi*

⅓–½ cup butter	2–2¼ cups boiling stock (preferably chicken), or water with bouillon cubes
1 cup raw rice	Salt

Melt butter in a heavy casserole. Add rice and sauté, stirring, over medium heat for 3 minutes or until butter is bubbly. Add boiling stock and salt and stir. Cover casserole and simmer, without stirring, for about 20 minutes, or until rice has absorbed all the liquid. A linen towel may be placed over the casserole after rice is cooked to absorb the excess moisture. Replace cover and allow casserole to stand a little longer. *4–6 servings*

Note: Finely chopped onion and fine noodles may be added with rice to melted butter and sautéed as above. One tablespoon tomato paste or ½ cup tomato sauce may be added to stock if a tomato flavor is desired. Do not increase amount of liquid.

RICE PILAF II *Rizi Pilafi*

2 cups water	Salt
1 tablespoon tomato paste	1 cup raw rice
(optional)	½ cup butter

Bring water to a boil, salt, and stir in tomato paste, if desired. Add rice and cook for about 20 minutes or until rice is tender. Cover rice with a linen towel to absorb excess moisture. Melt butter until it bubbles and pour over the rice. Toss rice with a fork to mix butter evenly. Serve immediately. *4–6 servings*

SALADS

GREEK SALAD *Salata*

The traditional Greek salad consists of greens (lettuce, chickory, escarole, romaine, endive, *etc.*), chopped or torn into bite-sized pieces, wedges of tomato, slices of cucumber, green pepper, chopped scallions or sliced onions, radishes, chopped parsley, anchovies, black olives, and feta cheese.* Any or all of these ingredients may be used. A large wooden salad bowl is rubbed with garlic. The dressing consists of 1 part lemon juice or wine vinegar to 3 parts olive oil, and salt and pepper. A sprinkling of oregano and dried mint may be added. Fresh mint in season gives the salad a delightful flavor.

ARTICHOKE TOSSED SALAD *Salata Anginarokardoules*

1 package frozen artichoke
    hearts
1 tomato, quartered
½ head lettuce, shredded
2 stalks celery, diced

1 small onion, sliced
Salt and pepper
Lemon and oil dressing, or a
    favorite salad dressing

Cook artichokes according to directions on package. Quarter them and add tomatoes, lettuce, celery, and onion. Sprinkle with salt and pepper. Toss with dressing and serve. *4 servings*

BEAN SALAD, POLITIKO STYLE *Fassoulia Piaz Politika*

½ pound navy pea beans
Water
2 onions, thinly sliced
½–1 cup olive oil

2 lemons, juice of
Salt and pepper
2–3 stalks celery, diced
½ cup parsley, chopped

Soak beans overnight; drain. Cover with fresh unsalted water, bring to a boil, and cook beans until soft. Drain. Place beans in a large bowl and add onions, olive oil, lemon juice, salt and pepper, celery, and parsley. Mix well and serve at room temperature or slightly chilled. *6–8 servings*

Note: Canned cannellini beans may be used in this recipe.

BEET SALAD *Pantzaria Salata*

2 1-pound cans cut red beets
    or 2 pounds cooked sliced
    fresh beets
5–6 cloves garlic, minced

½ cup olive oil
½ cup vinegar
Salt and pepper
Dash of monosodium glutamate

Combine ingredients and allow to marinate several hours before serving. This salad should be quite spicy, so add enough salt and pepper. *6–8 servings*

CUCUMBER SALAD *Angourosalata*

2 cucumbers, diced
4 cloves garlic, minced
½ cup olive oil

¼ cup vinegar
Salt and pepper
Dash of monosodium glutamate

Combine cucumbers and garlic. Add olive oil, vinegar, salt and pepper, and glutamate. Mix well. This salad tastes much better if prepared a few hours before serving. *4–6 servings*

EGGPLANT SALAD *Salata Melitzanas*

1 large eggplant	1½ tablespoons vinegar
1 small onion, chopped	Parsley, chopped
Salt and pepper	Tomato wedges
½ cup olive oil	Black olives

Bake eggplant in a moderate 350-degree oven for about 1 hour or until soft. Remove skin and chop flesh. In a bowl combine eggplant, onion, salt and pepper, olive oil, and vinegar and mix well. Garnish with chopped parsley, tomato wedges, and black olives. *6–8 servings*

GREEK HOT POTATO SALAD *Zesti Patatosalata*

4–5 large potatoes, peeled	2 lemons, juice of
Boiling salted water	½ cup diced celery
1 large onion	Salt and pepper
Salt and cold water	Parsley, chopped
½ cup olive oil	

Cook potatoes in boiling salted water until tender. Drain and keep hot. Slice onion into a large bowl. Sprinkle with salt and cold water and allow to stand for about 5 minutes; drain. Slice hot potatoes into bowl with onion. Add olive oil, lemon juice, and celery. Mix well to distribute dressing. Season to taste and garnish with chopped parsley. Serve warm. *6–8 servings*

STRING BEAN SALAD *Fassoulakia Salata*

1 pound string beans, French- style, fresh or frozen	1 lemon, juice of
	Salt and pepper to taste
¼ cup olive oil	1 onion, sliced into thin rings

Cook string beans until tender; drain. Add olive oil, lemon juice, and salt and pepper. Mix well and garnish with onion rings. This salad may be served either hot or cold. *4–6 servings*

TOMATO SALAD *Domatosalata*

2 medium onions
1 tablespoon salt
Cold water
5–6 ripe tomatoes

2 teaspoons oregano
¼ cup olive oil
Salt to taste

Cut onions in half and slice thinly lengthwise. Sprinkle slices with the 1 tablespoon salt, cover with cold water, and soak for 5 minutes. Drain. Wash tomatoes and cut into small pieces. Add onion slices, oregano, olive oil, and salt. Toss lightly. Let salad marinate at least 1 hour before serving. *8–10 servings*

DESSERTS

DESSERTS

Greek cakes and pastries can only be summed up as fabulous! Each, in sweet succession, is an epicurean delight. Here, the delicate, tissue-thin phyllo pastry* sheets are combined with nuts, baked to golden perfection, and bathed in Hymettos honey—the sweetest honey in the world, which the bees gather amid the fig trees and wild flowers along the ravines and across the hills surrounding Athens.

Such pastries are not really considered desserts in Greece. Usually a piece of fruit concludes a meal. But, since dinner is served late, afternoon coffee with a sweet of some kind is always served to appease the appetite. The women gather in the homes; the men congregate in the *kafenion,* or coffee shop, to relax and enjoy a rich pastry as they sip their cups of Turkish coffee.

Name days, weddings, and feast days are other occasions for serving sweets, and there are special pastries for each holiday. Christmas is synonymous with kourabiedes,* or Greek shortbread. New Year's Day is celebrated with the traditional vasilopeta,* and Easter brings forth koulourakia* and tsourekia.*

The recipes are all here and, although they may seem lavish and time-consuming to American homemakers, they are well worth the effort.

CAKES

APRICOT CHOCOLATE CUSTARD CAKE
Pantespani me Krema Tsokolatas

5 eggs	Chocolate custard (below)
1 cup sugar	1-pound jar apricot preserves
½ teaspoon salt	Chocolate sprinkles or finely
1 teaspoon vanilla	shaved chocolate
1¼ cups flour, sifted	

Grease two 9-inch layer cake pans, line with waxed paper, and grease again. Beat eggs until light. Gradually beat in sugar, salt, and vanilla and continue to beat until batter is thick and takes some time to level out when beater is withdrawn. Use an electric beater for this if possible. Carefully fold in flour, 2 tablespoons at a time, mixing until blended after each addition. Pour batter into cake pans and bake in a 350-degree oven for 25 minutes. Cool and split layers. Spread chocolate custard between the layers. Spread top and sides of cake with apricot preserves and cover sides with chocolate sprinkles or finely shaved chocolate. Chill in refrigerator until ready to serve. *10–12 servings*

Chocolate Custard:

¾ cup sugar	1 1-ounce square bitter
2 tablespoons cornstarch	chocolate, shaved
3 eggs	1 teaspoon vanilla
1½ cups milk	½ cup soft butter

In saucepan combine sugar and cornstarch. Add eggs and blend well with a fork. Stir in milk and cook over low heat, stirring constantly, until thick. Remove from heat and stir in shaved chocolate and vanilla. Cover and cool. Cream butter and gradually add the cooled chocolate mixture. Blend well.

ORANGE CAKE *Pantespani Portokali*

1 cup sugar
5 eggs, separated
½ pound butter, melted
1 orange, grated rind and
    juice of

1 cup flour
3½ teaspoons baking powder
Syrup (below)

Mix sugar and egg yolks well. Stir in melted butter, rind and juice of the orange, flour, and baking powder. Carefully fold in egg whites, stiffly beaten. Pour into a buttered 8×10-inch or 9×9-inch baking pan. Bake in a 375-degree oven for 10 minutes, lower oven temperature to 350 degrees, and bake for 30 minutes longer or until cake tests done. Cool, then pour hot syrup over the cake, cut into square- or diamond-shaped serving pieces, and serve. *16 servings*

Syrup:

2 cups water
1 cup sugar

2 jiggers orange curaçao or 2
    teaspoons orange extract

Combine water and sugar. Bring to a boil and boil for 10 minutes. Add orange curaçao or orange extract.

CREAM TORTE *Torta me Krema*

1 box, net weight 6 ounces,
    zwieback, ground
½ cup butter, melted
½ cup sugar
1 teaspoon cinnamon
5 cups milk

5 teaspoons cornstarch
5 tablespoons sugar
6 egg yolks
Pinch salt
1 teaspoon vanilla
6 egg whites, stiffly beaten

Combine zwieback crumbs, melted butter, sugar, and cinnamon. Reserve 1 cup of this crumb mixture and press remaining crumbs onto bottom and sides of a 9×11×2-inch cake pan. Heat 4 cups of the milk. In a saucepan combine cornstarch, sugar, egg yolks, salt, and the remaining cup of milk. Gradually stir in hot milk. Cook over low heat, stirring constantly, for about 8 minutes or until custard thickens. Add vanilla. Pour custard mixture into prepared pan. Spread beaten egg whites evenly over the custard, sprinkle with reserved crumb mixture, and bake in a 350-degree over for 40 to 45 minutes. Cool and cut into squares. *24 servings*

GALOPETA (Custard Cake) I

5½ cups milk	8 eggs
2 cups sugar	½ cup water
1 cup butter	1 orange, grated rind of
11 ounces cream of wheat or	5–6 phyllo pastry sheets
farina (1½ cups)	Melted butter

In a saucepan combine milk, sugar, butter, and farina. Bring to a boil and cook over low heat, stirring constantly, until thick and smooth. Cool. Beat eggs with the water and stir in grated orange rind. Combine with cool farina mixture. Line a 9×11×2-inch cake pan with 5 or 6 phyllo pastry sheets, brushing each generously with melted butter. Pour in the egg-farina mixture and bake in a moderate 350-degree oven for about 40 minutes or until set. Cut into squares and serve warm. *20 servings*

GALATOPETA (Custard Cake) II

1 quart milk	6 eggs
¾ cup sugar plus 2 tablespoons	Cinnamon
½ cup farina plus 2 tablespoons	Chopped nuts
½ cup butter plus 2 tablespoons	

In a saucepan combine milk and sugar and bring to a boil. Gradually stir in farina. Stir in 2 tablespoons of the butter and cook, stirring constantly, until thickened. Remove from heat. Beat eggs well and gradually beat in farina mixture. In a 9×13×2-inch pan heat remaining ½ cup butter until golden brown. Pour in the farina-egg mixture and bake in a moderate 350-degree oven for about 30 minutes or until a knife inserted comes out clean. Remove from oven and sprinkle with cinnamon and chopped nuts. Serve warm if possible. *20–24 servings*

GALATOBOUREKO

Omit cinnamon and nuts from recipe above. Line baking pan with 8 or 10 sheets of buttered phyllo pastry before pouring in the farina-egg mixture. Top with 8 or 10 additional buttered phyllo pastry sheets. Bake, cool, and pour over a hot syrup made by combining 3 cups sugar, 2 cups water, and 1 slice lemon and boiling for 10 minutes.

GOLDEN NUT-MERINGUE CAKE *Melachrino Xantho*

½ *pound sweet butter*	1½ *cups flour*
1½ *cups sugar*	2½ *teaspoons baking powder*
4 *eggs*	1 *jigger cognac*
6 *egg yolks (use whites for*	¼ *cup milk*
meringue)	*Meringue (below)*
1 *lemon, grated rind of*	*Syrup (below)*

Cream butter until light and gradually beat in sugar. Beat eggs and egg yolks until light and gradually beat into the creamed mixture. Stir in grated lemon rind. Sift together flour and baking powder and stir into the egg mixture alternately with the cognac and milk. Pour batter into a buttered 10×14×2-inch pan and bake in a moderate 350-degree oven for about 40 minutes or until cake tests done. Remove from oven and cool. Spread meringue-nut mixture over cooled cake, return to a slow 300-degree oven, and bake for 15 to 20 minutes or until meringue is browned. Cool cake again and, when cool, pour hot syrup over it, cover with another pan, cover pan with a cloth, and let stand until cool. Cut into squares to serve. This cake is best if made 3 or 4 days in advance of serving. *30 servings*

Meringue:

6 *egg whites*	1½ *pounds walnut meats,*
1 *cup sugar*	*chopped*
2 *teaspoons lemon juice*	

Beat egg whites until they stand in soft peaks. Gradually beat in the sugar and continue to beat until meringue is glossy. Beat in lemon juice and fold in the chopped nuts.

Syrup:

Combine ½ cup sugar and 1 cup water. Bring to a boil and boil for 10 minutes or until of medium consistency.

NUT CAKE I *Karidopeta I*

12 *eggs, separated*	¾ *pound (3 cups) blanched*
1½ *cups sugar*	*ground almonds*
1 *teaspoon vanilla*	16 *pieces zwieback, finely*
¾ *pound (3 cups) shelled*	*crushed*
ground walnuts	1 *orange, grated rind of*
	Rum syrup (below)

Grease a 16×13×3-inch pan. Beat egg whites until stiff and set aside. Beat yolks with sugar until thick and pale in color. Beat in vanilla. Mix nuts, zwieback, and rind together. Gradually fold beaten egg whites into yolk mixture and fold in nut mixture. Pour batter into prepared pan and bake in a 350-degree oven for exactly 1 hour. While cake is baking, make the syrup. Pour the syrup over the cake the moment it is taken from the oven. Cool and, before serving, cut into diamond-shaped serving pieces. *Yield: 48 pieces*

Note: If desired, the recipe may be halved and baked in 13×9× 2-inch pan. Or it may be reduced by ⅓ and baked in a 10×14×2-inch pan.

Rum Syrup:

2 cups sugar
4½ cups water
1 stick cinnamon

1 slice lemon
½ cup light rum

In a saucepan combine sugar, water, cinnamon, and lemon. Bring to a boil and simmer until sugar is dissolved. Remove from heat and stir in rum. *Yield: about 5½ cups*

NUT CAKE II *Karidopeta II*

14 eggs, separated
3 cups sugar
1 box, net weight 6-ounces, zwieback, finely ground

1 pound walnut meats, finely ground
1 teaspoon cinnamon
2 teaspoons baking powder
Confectioners' sugar

Beat egg yolks and sugar until thick and pale in color. Beat egg whites until they stand in soft peaks. Fold egg yolk mixture into egg whites alternately with the zwieback. Fold in walnuts, cinnamon, and baking powder. Turn mixture into a well-buttered 10×14×2-inch pan and bake in a hot 450-degree oven for 10 minutes. Reduce oven temperature to 375 degrees and continue to bake for 40 to 45 minutes longer or until a tester comes out clean. Cool and just before serving sprinkle generously with confectioners' sugar. *30 servings*

NUT CAKE III *Karidopeta III*

1 cup butter	2½ cups flour, sifted
1½ cups sugar	2 teaspoons baking powder
5 eggs	1 cup walnuts, chopped
1 teaspoon cinnamon	Syrup (below)

Cream butter and sugar together. Add eggs, one at a time, and beat well after each addition. Stir in cinnamon, flour, and baking powder. Stir in walnuts. Turn batter into a greased 10×14×2-inch pan and bake in a hot 425-degree oven for 30 to 35 minutes or until cake tests done. Remove from oven and, while hot, pour cool syrup over it. Cut into diamond shapes. *30 servings*

Syrup:

Combine 2¾ cups water and 1¾ cups sugar. Bring to a boil and boil for 10 minutes. Cool.

ALMOND TORTE *Tourta Me Amygthala*

12 eggs, separated	1 box, net weight 6 ounces,
1½ cups sugar	zwieback, crumbed
1½ cups blanched almonds,	1 teaspoon almond extract
finely chopped	½ pound butter
	Syrup (below)

Beat egg yolks until light and gradually beat in sugar. Fold in almonds, zwieback, and almond extract. Beat egg whites until stiff and fold into egg yolk mixture. Melt butter until hot and sizzling and fold into cake batter. Pour batter into a buttered 10×14×2-inch pan and bake in a slow 325-degree oven for 40 to 45 minutes or until cake tests done. Remove from oven and pour hot syrup over hot cake. *30 servings*

Syrup:

Combine 2½ cups sugar, 3 cups water, and lemon juice and cinnamon to taste. Bring to a boil and boil for 10 to 15 minutes.

NUT CAKE *Karidopeta*

1 cup butter	3 cups ground nut meats
1 cup confectioners' sugar	(almonds, walnuts, and/or
1 cup flour	pecans)
7 eggs, separated	⅓ cup dry bread crumbs
1 cup sugar	1 teaspoon vanilla

Cream butter and confectioners' sugar until light and fluffy. Stir in enough flour to make a pastry dough that can be rolled out. Roll out thinly on a lightly floured board and cut to fit a 9-inch angel food pan. Line pan with the pastry.

Beat egg yolks and sugar until light and pale in color. Fold in nuts, bread crumbs, and vanilla. Beat egg whites until stiff but not dry and fold into egg yolk mixture. Turn mixture into lined pan and bake in a moderate 350-degree oven for 1 hour. *16 servings*

PASTA FLEURA I

1 cup butter	¼ cup milk
½ cup sugar	1 jigger brandy
3 egg yolks, beaten	3½–4 cups flour
1 teaspoon vanilla or almond	1-pound jar cherry preserves
extract	1 egg white, lightly beaten
½ teaspoon baking powder	

Cream butter and sugar together. Add egg yolks and vanilla or almond extract and mix well. Stir in baking powder, mixed with the milk, and the brandy. Stir in enough flour to make a soft dough. Roll out two thirds of the dough thinly on a floured board and line a buttered, shallow, 10×14-inch pan, or pat dough thinly into pan. Cover dough with cherry preserves. Roll out remaining dough thinly and cut into long strips. Cover preserves with a lattice topping of the strips. Brush with egg white and bake in a moderate 350- to 375-degree oven for 45 minutes. Cut into squares and remove from pan while warm. *40–60 servings*

PASTA FLEURA II

1 cup butter	1 cup corn meal or additional 1
2 cups sugar	cup flour
2½ teaspoons baking powder	4 eggs
4 cups flour	1 pound dried apricots
	Beaten egg

Cream butter and sugar together until light and fluffy. Sift baking powder and flour together and add to butter mixture with the corn meal or additional flour. Add eggs and mix to make a firm dough. Butter a shallow 10×14-inch pan and press ¾ of the dough mixture over bottom and sides. Cook apricots according to directions on package and mash. Arrange apricot pulp on top of dough. Roll out remaining dough and cut into thin strips. Cover apricots with a lattice topping of the strips. Brush with beaten egg and bake in a 350-degree oven for about 1 hour or until pastry is golden. *30 servings*

RAVANI I

1 cup butter	2 cups self-rising flour
¾ cup sugar	3 teaspoons baking powder
5 eggs, beaten	2 teaspoons vanilla
1 cup regular farina	Syrup (below)

Melt butter over low heat. Add sugar and cream together until light and fluffy. Beat in eggs. Stir in farina alternately with the flour. Stir in baking powder and vanilla. Beat well. Turn into a greased 10×14×2-inch pan and bake in a 350-degree oven for 30 to 35 minutes or until cake tests done. Cut cake into squares and pour the cool syrup over it. *30 servings*

Syrup:

Combine 3 cups water and 2 cups sugar. Bring to a boil and boil for 15 minutes. Cool.

RAVANI II

7 egg whites	Orange rind, grated
1 cup sugar	2 cups self-rising flour
1 cup butter	¼ cup regular farina
7 egg yolks, beaten	Syrup (below)
1 teaspoon vanilla	Whipped cream

Beat egg whites until stiff. Gradually beat in ½ cup of the sugar to make a glossy meringue. In another bowl beat butter with remaining sugar until light and fluffy. Add egg yolks, vanilla, and orange rind and beat well. Gradually stir in flour and farina, mixing until smooth after each addition. Fold in meringue. Turn batter into a greased 10×14×2-inch pan and bake in a 350-degree oven for 35 to 40 minutes or until cake tests done. Cool a little, then pour the hot syrup over the cake. Cut into diamond shapes and serve with whipped cream. *30 servings*

Syrup:

Combine 2 cups sugar, 2½ cups water, and the juice of ½ lemon. Bring to a boil and boil for 5 minutes.

MOCK RAVANI

1 cup butter
1¼ cups sugar
4 large eggs, separated

2 cups self-rising flour
Syrup (below)

Cream butter well, add sugar, and cream until light and fluffy. Add egg yolks and beat well. Stir in flour, mixing until batter is smooth after each addition. Fold in stiffly beaten egg whites. Turn batter into a greased 8×12-inch pan and bake in a 350-degree oven for about 30 minutes or until cake tests done. Remove from oven and, while hot, pour over hot syrup. *12 servings*

Syrup:

Combine 2 cups sugar, 2 cups water, and lemon juice and cinnamon to taste. Bring to a boil and boil for 10 minutes.

RUM CAKE A LA GRECQUE   *Pantespani me Romion*

10 eggs, separated
½ cup sugar
*1½ cups toasted blanched
 almonds, chopped*
½ cup cake flour
1 tablespoon baking powder

*2 teaspoons rum flavoring or 3
 tablespoons rum*
Syrup (below)
1 teaspoon sugar
2 cups heavy cream, whipped
Maraschino cherries

Beat egg yolks with the ½ cup sugar until thick and pale in color. Fold in 1 cup of the chopped almonds. Fold in flour mixed with baking powder. Stir in rum flavoring or rum. Beat egg whites until stiff but not dry and carefully fold into egg yolk batter. Turn batter into a greased 8×12×2-inch pan and bake in a preheated 400-degree oven for about 30 minutes or until cake tests done. Remove cake from oven and prick entire surface with a toothpick. While cake is still hot, pour the hot syrup over it and cool. When cool, fold the 1 teaspoon sugar into the whipped cream and frost cake lavishly. Cut into 2-inch squares and sprinkle with remaining almonds. Decorate with cherries. *24 servings*

Syrup:

Combine 3 cups sugar, 2½ cups water, and juice of ½ lemon. Bring to a boil and boil for 10 minutes. Then add 1 teaspoon rum flavoring or 1 tablespoon rum.

CHRISTMAS BREAD   *Christopsomo*

4 cakes or packages yeast	*¾ cup sugar*
1 cup lukewarm water	*½ teaspoon salt*
1 cup warm milk	*¼ teaspoon ground masticha**
1 pound sweet butter, melted and cooled	*Walnut halves*
4 pounds flour (about 16 cups)	*Beaten egg*
8 eggs	*Sesame seeds*

Soften yeast in lukewarm water. Stir in milk. Blend butter with flour thoroughly and stir in eggs, sugar, salt, and *masticha*. Stir in yeast mixture and mix well. Turn out on lightly floured board and knead for 10 minutes until dough is smooth and elastic. Place dough in oiled bowl, cover with cloth, and let rise in a warm place for about 2 hours or until double in bulk. Punch down and knead until smooth. Take a small piece of dough and roll out, making 2 crosses. Form remaining dough into 2 loaves and put into large floured bread pans. Put a cross on top of each loaf and press walnut halves along the edges of each cross. Cover pans and let dough rise in a warm place for about 1½ hours or until double in bulk. Brush tops with beaten egg, sprinkle with sesame seeds, and bake in a 350-degree oven for 45 minutes or until bread is golden brown. *Yield: 2 loaves*

NEW YEAR'S CAKE I *Vasilopeta*

½ cup milk	3 eggs, beaten
½ cup sugar plus 2 tablespoons	About 6 cups sifted flour
1 teaspoon salt	1 tablespoon ground mahlepi*
¾ cup butter, melted and cooled	Melted butter
¼ cup lukewarm water	Beaten egg
2 tablespoons sugar	Sesame seeds
2 packages yeast	Blanched almonds

Scald milk. Stir in the ½ cup plus 2 tablespoons sugar, salt, and butter. Cool to lukewarm. Measure into a bowl the lukewarm water and the 2 tablespoons sugar. Sprinkle in the yeast. Let stand until softened, 5 to 10 minutes. Stir in the lukewarm milk mixture. Stir in the beaten eggs. Slowly add and stir in 3 cups of the flour. Beat until smooth. Add the *mahlepi*. Add and stir in an additional 2 to 3 cups flour. Turn out dough on a lightly floured board and knead until smooth.

Place dough in a greased bowl and brush top lightly with melted butter. Cover with a clean towel and let rise in a warm place, free from drafts, until dough has doubled in bulk, about 1 hour and 25 minutes. Punch down dough and knead lightly. Form into two 9-inch cakes. Place in cake pans, cover with a clean towel, and let the cakes rise in a warm place for about 1 hour. When cakes have risen, brush tops with beaten egg, sprinkle with sesame seeds, and decorate with blanched almonds. Bake in a 375-degree preheated oven for 40 to 45 minutes or until cakes are a deep golden brown. Cool. *Yield: 2 9-inch cakes*

Note: When making this recipe for New Year's Eve, it is customary to place a silver coin in each cake for luck. This coin may be added when the cakes are shaped and placed in pans for final rising.

NEW YEAR'S CAKE II *Vasilopeta*

½ pound butter	1 cup lukewarm milk
2 cups sugar	½ teaspoon baking soda
3 cups flour	½ lemon, juice of
6 eggs	Chopped nuts
2 teaspoons baking powder	Sugar

Cream butter and sugar together until light. Add flour and stir until mixture is mealy. Add eggs, one at a time, beating well after each addition. Stir baking powder into milk and stir milk into the egg mixture. Mix soda and lemon juice and stir in. Mix well. Pour batter into a greased layer cake pan 10 inches in diameter and 2 inches deep. Bake in a moderate 350-degree oven for 20 minutes. Sprinkle with nuts and sugar and continue baking for 20 to 30 minutes longer or until cake tests done. *Yield: 1 10-inch cake*

PETA

2 cakes or packages yeast
¼ cup lukewarm water
3½ pounds (about 14 cups) flour
2 teaspoons baking soda
2 teaspoons cinnamon
1 teaspoon masticha*

1 pound butter, melted and cooled
1¾ pounds (3½ cups) sugar
2½ cups water
Beaten egg
Sesame seeds
Blanched almonds

Soften yeast in the lukewarm water. Beat in enough of the flour to make a thin batter and let rise for about 2 hours. In a large mixing bowl combine remaining flour, baking soda, cinnamon, and *masticha*. Stir in melted butter. Dissolve sugar in the water and stir into flour mixture along with the yeast. Turn out on lightly floured board and knead until dough is smooth and elastic. Put into a greased bowl, cover, and let rise in a warm place for about 1½ hours or until double in bulk. Divide dough in half. Mold each half into a cake and put into greased pans. Cover with towel and let rise until double in bulk. Brush tops with beaten egg, sprinkle with sesame seeds, and decorate with almonds. Press cakes along edges with tines of a fork to make a fluted effect. Bake in a 350-degree oven for about 1 hour or until golden. Keep covered with waxed paper for the first ½ hour to prevent tops from overbrowning. Uncover and complete the baking. *Yield: 2 9-inch cakes*

EASTER BREAD *Lambropsomo*

4 cakes or packages yeast
1 cup lukewarm water
1 cup warm milk
½ pound butter, melted and cooled
4 pounds flour
5 eggs, beaten

¼ cup sugar
Dash salt
½ teaspoon ground masticha*
10 eggs, dyed red
Beaten egg
Sesame seeds

Soften yeast in the lukewarm water. Stir in milk. Blend butter with flour and stir in eggs, sugar, salt, and *masticha*. Add yeast mixture and blend thoroughly. Turn out on lightly floured board and knead for 10 minutes or until dough is smooth and elastic. Put into greased bowl, cover, and let rise in a warm place for about 2 hours or until double in bulk. Punch down dough and knead again until smooth. Divide in half and form each half into a loaf. Place loaves in large floured pans and make 5 depressions in each, 1 in the center and the others at the 4 opposite edges of the dough. Place eggs in these depressions. Cover pans and let dough rise for about 1½ hours or until double in bulk. Brush tops with beaten egg and sprinkle with sesame seeds. Bake in a 350-degree oven for 45 minutes or until bread is golden. *Yield: 2 loaves*

EASTER TWIST *Tsoureki*

5 pounds (20 cups) flour
3½–4 cups sugar
1 tablespoon salt
3 teaspoons powdered
    mahlepi*
10 eggs, well beaten

2 cups sweet butter, melted
2 cups lukewarm milk
2 cakes or packages yeast
1 cup lukewarm water
1–2 eggs, beaten
Sesame seeds

Sift flour into a large bowl and combine with sugar, salt, and *mahlepi*. Make a well in the center and into the well pour the 10 beaten eggs, butter, milk, and the yeast softened in the lukewarm water. Blend liquids gradually into flour mixture, first with a spoon, then with the hands. Turn dough out on a lightly floured board and knead for 15 to 20 minutes or until smooth. Cover dough and let stand for 4 to 5 hours or overnight. Punch down and form dough into twists with floured hands. To do this, take three long ropes of the dough, press ends together, braid, and fasten opposite ends. Brush with beaten egg and sprinkle with sesame seeds. Place on greased baking sheets and bake in a 350-degree oven 40 minutes for large twists, 30 minutes for small. *Yield: 4 large twists or 8 small twists*

YOGURT CAKE *Yiaourtopeta*

½ cup butter	½ teaspoon baking soda
2 cups sugar	Pinch of salt
2 eggs	1 cup yogurt
2½ cups flour	Syrup (below)

Cream butter and sugar together. Beat in eggs. Sift flour, soda, and salt together and add to butter mixture alternately with the yogurt. Turn batter into a greased 10×14-inch pan or an angel food pan and bake in a 375-degree oven for 30 to 40 minutes or until cake tests done. Remove from oven and pour cool syrup over the hot cake. *Yield: 30 pieces*

Syrup:

Combine 2¾ cups water and 1¾ cups sugar. Bring to a boil and boil for 10 minutes. Cool.

YOGURT PIE *Yiaourtopeta*

½ pound cream cheese	1 teaspoon vanilla
1 cup yogurt	1 baked pie shell or graham
3 tablespoons honey	cracker crust

Have cream cheese at room temperature and cream well. Add yogurt, a little at a time, mixing until smooth. Stir in honey and vanilla. Pour into baked pie shell and refrigerate for at least 24 hours before serving. *8 servings*

COOKIES

BUTTER COOKIES I *Koulourakia*

1 cup sweet butter	1 teaspoon salt
½ cup vegetable shortening	½ teaspoon cinnamon or nutmeg
2 cups sugar	1 cup heavy cream
2 eggs, beaten	2 teaspoons vanilla
6 cups flour	Beaten egg
4 teaspoons baking powder	Sesame seeds

Cream butter and shortening until fluffy. Gradually beat in sugar. Beat in eggs. Sift together flour, baking powder, salt, and spice, and stir into the egg mixture alternately with the cream and vanilla. Shape dough with floured hands into desired shapes. Brush with beaten egg and sprinkle with sesame seeds. Place on cooky sheets and bake in a moderate 350-degree oven for about 15 minutes or until golden brown. *Yield: 6–8 dozen small cookies*

BUTTER COOKIES II *Koulourakia*

2 cups (1 pound) butter
2 cups sugar
6 eggs
1 teaspoon vanilla

8–9 cups flour, sifted
2 tablespoons baking powder
1 egg beaten with 1 tablespoon water

Cream butter and gradually beat in sugar. Beat eggs until light; add to butter mixture and beat thoroughly. Add vanilla. Sift flour and baking powder. Carefully blend into butter-egg mixture to make a soft dough. Shape dough with lightly floured hands into desired shapes and arrange on cooky sheets. Brush cookies with beaten egg and water. Bake in a 375-degree oven for 20 minutes or until golden brown. *Yield: 8–10 dozen small cookies*

BUTTER COOKIES III *Koulourakia*

2 cups (1 pound) sweet butter
1½ cups sugar
3 eggs, beaten
1 jigger whiskey
½ cup salad oil

3 pounds (12 cups) flour
7 teaspoons baking powder
Beaten egg
Sesame seeds

Cream butter until fluffy and gradually beat in sugar. Beat in eggs and whiskey and stir in salad oil. Sift together flour and baking powder and gradually stir into the egg mixture to make a soft dough. Shape dough with floured hands into desired shapes. Arrange on cooky sheets. Brush with beaten egg, sprinkle with sesame seeds, and bake in a 350-degree oven for 15 minutes or until golden. *Yield: 10 dozen small cookies*

SESAME COOKIES *Koulourakia me Sousame*

2 cups (1 pound) butter	6 cups flour, sifted
1 cup sugar	1 egg beaten with 1 tablespoon
1 cup milk	water
2 teaspoons baking powder	Sesame seeds
½ teaspoon cinnamon	

Cream butter and gradually beat in sugar. Add milk, baking powder, and cinnamon and mix well. Slowly stir in flour until a soft dough is formed. Shape dough with floured hands into small rings (miniature doughnuts). Dip each ring into egg mixture, then dip in a dish of sesame seeds, carefully covering cookies on all sides. Place on cooky sheets and bake in a 350-degree oven for 20 minutes or until golden brown. *Yield: 6–8 dozen small cookies*

HONEY-DIPPED COOKIES I *Fenikia*

1 cup peanut oil	1 tablespoon cinnamon
1 cup (½ pound) butter	1 tablespoon clove
⅔ cup water	1 cup walnuts, chopped
1 jigger brandy or cognac	½ cup sugar
2 eggs, beaten	Dash each cinnamon and clove
3 cups flour	Syrup (below)
2½ teaspoons baking powder	Chopped walnuts for garnish

Heat oil and butter over low heat until butter is melted and mixture is hot. Remove from heat and stir in water and brandy. Cool. Stir in beaten eggs. Sift together flour and baking powder with the tablespoon each cinnamon and clove and stir into mixture to make a dough that is not too soft. Add a little more flour if necessary. With floured hands shaped dough into ovals and indent lengthwise with thumbs. Combine chopped walnuts with sugar and dash each cinnamon and clove. Put 1 teaspoon of this filling into the indentation in the dough and close dough over filling. Place on cooky sheets and bake in a 400-degree oven for about 25 minutes or until golden brown. Cool. Dip cooled cookies into hot syrup and place on racks to drain. Decorate with chopped walnuts. *Yield: 6 dozen small cookies*

Syrup:

Combine 2 cups sugar, 1 cup water, 1 pound honey, and lemon slices. Bring to a boil and boil for 5 minutes.

HONEY-DIPPED COOKIES II *Fenikia*

7 *cups flour*
2 *heaping tablespoons baking*
powder
2 *cups vegetable oil*
1 *cup butter, melted*
1 *cup orange juice*

1 *cup sugar*
½ *cup walnuts, chopped*
1 *ounce cognac or brandy*
Syrup (below)
Chopped nuts

Sift together flour and baking powder. In a large bowl combine oil and melted butter. Add orange juice, sugar, ½ cup chopped nuts, and cognac. Gradually mix flour into oil-and-butter mixture by hand and knead until a dough is formed that does not stick to the hands. Add more flour if necessary. Shape into small ovals, place on ungreased baking sheets, and bake in a 400-degree oven for 10 minutes. Lower oven temperature to 325 degrees and continue to bake for 25 minutes longer or until well browned. Keep syrup simmering while adding 7 or 8 cookies at a time. Allow them to remain in syrup for 2 to 3 minutes, remove, and place again on baking sheets to drain. Sprinkle with chopped nuts at once. Store in airtight tins when cooled. These cookies may be baked in advance and stored, and dipped into syrup as needed. *Yield: 12 dozen small cookies*

Syrup:

Combine a 12-ounce jar honey, 2 cups sugar, 1½ cups water, and juice of ½ lemon. Bring to a boil and boil for 15 minutes.

KOURABIEDES I

2 *cups (1 pound) sweet butter*
3 *tablespoons confectioners'*
sugar
2 *egg yolks, lightly beaten*
1 *jigger brandy or Scotch*
whiskey

1 *cup walnuts or blanched*
almonds, chopped
1 *teaspoon baking powder*
4½ *cups flour, sifted*
Confectioners' sugar for topping

Cream butter until light, beating for 15 minutes. Beat in sugar, egg yolks, flavoring, and nuts. Sift baking powder and flour and carefully blend into butter mixture. Shape into small crescents. Place on baking sheets and bake in a 425-degree oven for 15 to 20 minutes. Sift confectioners' sugar on a large sheet of waxed paper. Place cookies on the sugar and sift additional sugar over tops and sides. Cool thoroughly before storing. *Yield: 10 dozen small crescents*

KOURABIEDES II

2 cups (1 pound) sweet butter
½ cup confectioners' sugar
2 egg yolks, lightly beaten
⅔ cup blanched almonds, finely
  chopped

1½ ounces brandy
⅓ cup orange juice
1 teaspoon baking powder
4½–5 cups flour, sifted
Confectioners' sugar for topping

Cream butter until very light. Beat in sugar, egg yolks, almonds, brandy, and orange juice. Sift baking powder with flour and carefully blend into butter mixture. Shape into small crescents and place on baking sheets. Bake in a 400-degree oven for 20 minutes. Sift confectioners' sugar onto a large sheet of waxed paper. Upon removing cookies from oven, carefully place on sugar and sift additional sugar over tops and sides. Cool thoroughly before storing. *Yield: 10 dozen small crescents*

KOURABIEDES III

2 cups sweet butter
¾ cup confectioners' sugar
1 egg yolk
1 jigger brandy or cognac

4½ cups sifted flour
Whole cloves
Confectioners' sugar for topping

Cream butter until very light. Gradually beat in sugar. Beat in egg yolk and brandy. Gradually blend in flour to make a soft dough. With floured hands shape dough into 1½-inch balls and stud each ball with 1 whole clove. Place on baking sheets and bake in a 350-degree oven for 15 minutes. Cool slightly and sift confectioners' sugar over cookies. *Yield: 4–6 dozen*

KOURABIEDES IV

1 pound sweet butter
3 tablespoons confectioners'
  sugar

2 egg yolks
5 cups flour, sifted
Confectioners' sugar for topping

Cream butter until very light and fluffy. Gradually beat in sugar. Add egg yolks and mix well. Gradually work in sifted flour to make a soft dough. With floured hands shape dough into small crescents and place about 1 inch apart on ungreased cooky sheets. Bake in a moderate 375-degree oven for about 20 minutes or until lightly browned. Test to see if cookies are done by breaking one in the center. If there is no butter line in the middle of the cooky, they are baked. Sift confectioners' sugar on a large sheet of waxed paper. Carefully place cookies on the sugar and sift additional sugar over tops and sides. Cool thoroughly before storing. *Yield: 10 dozen small crescents*

OLD-FASHIONED KOURABIEDES

2 cups (1 pound) sweet butter
Confectioners' sugar

1 teaspoon almond flavoring
Flour

Melt butter and bring to a boil. Skim off foam and carefully pour butter from pan into a small bowl, being careful not to include the sediment in bottom of pan. Refrigerate. When butter is solid, remove from bowl and, using butter line as measure, add enough confectioners' sugar to come to within 1 inch of this line. Cream butter until very light, add sugar, and beat well. Add almond flavoring and enough flour to form a soft dough. Shape dough with floured hands into small rounds, place on cooky sheets, and bake in a 350-degree oven for 15 to 20 minutes or until done but still light in color. These cookies are left unsugared. *Yield: 4 dozen cookies*

SWEET BISCUITS I *Paximadia*

1 cup vegetable oil
2 cups sugar
6 eggs, beaten
2 heaping teaspoons baking
  powder

1 cup almonds or walnuts,
  chopped
1 teaspoon vanilla
About 3 pounds (12 cups)
  flour

In a large bowl mix all ingredients, adding enough flour to make a dough that can be shaped. Pat into narrow loaves about 1 inch high and 6 to 8 inches long. Place on baking sheet and bake in a 350-degree oven for 30 minutes. Remove from oven and slice each loaf diagonally. Turn slices on their sides and return to oven. Continue to bake for 30 minutes longer. *Yield: 12–14 dozen biscuits*

SWEET BISCUITS II *Paximadia*

¾ cup butter
¾ cup sugar
3 eggs, beaten
½ cup almonds, chopped

2½ cups flour
½ tablespoon baking powder
1 teaspoon baking soda
1 tablespoon salad oil

Cream butter and beat in sugar gradually. Beat in beaten eggs and nuts. Sift dry ingredients together and mix into butter mixture gradually. Add salad oil. Pat into 3 loaves about 1 inch thick. Place loaves on baking sheet and bake in a 350-degree oven for 30 minutes. Remove from oven and slice. Turn slices on their sides, return to oven, and continue to bake for 30 minutes longer. *Yield: 4–6 dozen biscuits*

PECAN BARS *Karidata*

2 cups butter	4 cups flour
8 tablespoons confectioners' sugar	2 tablespoons vanilla
	2 tablespoons ice water
4 cups pecans, chopped	1 pound confectioners' sugar

Cream butter thoroughly. Gradually add the 8 tablespoons confectioners' sugar and continue creaming until well blended. Mix nuts and flour and add gradually to the creamed mixture. Add vanilla and ice water and mix well. Roll pieces of dough with palms of the hands into 1-inch rolls or crescents. Arrange on cooky sheets and bake in a 325-degree oven for 35 minutes or until golden brown. Sift confectioners' sugar generously over cookies and place in cooky jar to mellow. *Yield: 50–55 cookies*

CRETAN TURNOVERS *Skaltsounia*

½ pound feta cheese*	½ cup butter, softened
1 3-ounce package cream cheese	Pastry dough (below)
2 eggs, beaten	Oil or fat for frying (optional)
2 tablespoons dried mint leaves, crushed	Sugar or honey for topping

Combine cheese and eggs in a bowl and whip until smooth. Add mint and mix in butter. Set aside while making pastry.

Roll out dough on a floured board as thinly as possible. Cut dough into 3-inch rounds. Place 1 heaping tablespoon of filling on each round, fold over dough as in making turnovers, moisten edges, and seal. If desired, fry in olive oil or hot fat until light brown on both sides. Place on platter and sprinkle with sugar or dip in honey. Or, if preferred, turnovers may be placed on an ungreased baking sheet and baked in a 350-degree oven for 15 to 20 minutes or until golden, then sprinkled with sugar or dipped in honey. *Yield: approximately 3 dozen*

Pastry:

4 cups flour ½ cup shortening
½ teaspoon salt ½–1 cup cold water

Sift flour and salt into mixing bowl. Cut in shortening with pastry cutter or 2 knives. Stir in enough water to make a firm dough that can be gathered together.

NUT TURNOVERS Skaltsounia

1 cup walnut meats, coarsely chopped
1 cup blanched almonds coarsely chopped
1 teaspoon cinnamon
1 teaspoon clove
1 teaspoon masticha*
Honey
Pastry dough (recipe above)
Rose water or orange-flower water
Confectioners' sugar

Combine nuts, cinnamon, clove, and *masticha* and mix with enough honey to bind the mixture without making it too stiff. Allow to stand while making pastry. Roll out dough as thinly as possible on a floured board and cut into 3-inch rounds. Place 1 heaping tablespoon of filling on each round, fold over as in making an apple turnover, moisten edges, and seal. Place turnovers on a greased baking sheet and bake in a 400-degree oven for about 15 minutes or until golden brown. Remove from oven, let cool slightly, then dip in rose water or orange-flower water and sprinkle with sugar. *Yield: approximately 3 dozen*

ALMOND PEARS *Amygthalota*

1 pound blanched almonds
1 cup sugar
Vanilla extract to taste
3 egg whites, lightly beaten
½ cup soft bread crumbs
Cloves
Orange-flower water or rose water
Confectioners' sugar

Grind the almonds with 2 tablespoons of the sugar until very fine. Add remaining sugar, vanilla, egg whites, and bread crumbs. Knead to a form a dough. Shape small pieces of the dough into small pear shapes and insert a clove in each to represent the stems. Arrange on buttered baking sheet and bake in a 350-degree oven for 15 minutes. Cool. Dip each "pear" into orange-flower water or rose-water and dust generously with confectioners' sugar. *Yield: approximately 2 dozen*

PHYLLO PASTRY DESSERTS

COPENHAGEN I

Pastry dough (below)
15 eggs, separated
1 cup sugar
1½ pounds toasted blanched almonds, finely chopped
½ pound walnut meats, finely chopped

2 teaspoons baking powder
2 teaspoons cinnamon
2 teaspoons almond flavoring
1 jigger cognac
6–8 sheets phyllo pastry*
½ cup sweet butter, melted
Syrup (below)

Use a 16×20-inch rectangular pan or a 16-inch round pan, 2 inches deep. Pat pastry dough into the pan evenly and smoothly, bringing the edge up a little higher than edges of pan. Prick well with tines of a fork and bake in a 350-degree oven for 15 minutes or until golden brown. Cool. Beat egg yolks until light. Gradually beat in sugar and continue to beat until mixture is thick and pale in color. Fold in almonds, walnuts, baking powder, cinnamon, almond flavoring, and cognac. Beat egg whites until stiff but not dry and fold carefully into the egg yolk mixture. The mixture is difficult to handle with a mixing spoon, so use both hands to fold and blend. Turn mixture into the cool baked crust.

Brush each phyllo pastry sheet, one at a time, with melted butter and place the layers over the egg mixture. Make a few long slits in the pastry with a sharp knife and bake in a moderate 350-degree oven for about 1 hour or until a knife inserted into the filling comes out clean. Remove from oven and score in diamond-shaped or square serving pieces. Pour the cold syrup over the hot dessert. *60–80 servings*

Pastry Dough:

2 cups (1 pound) sweet butter
1 cup fine granulated sugar
3 egg yolks

Orange or lemon rind, grated
1 jigger cognac
Flour

Cream butter until very light. Gradually beat in sugar and beat until mixture is light and fluffy. Beat in egg yolks, one at a time, and beat for 2 minutes after each addition. Beat in grated orange or lemon rind and the cognac. Gradually stir in just enough flour to make a soft dough.

Syrup:

In saucepan combine 6 cups sugar, 3 cups water, 1 small jar honey, and juice of ½ lemon. Bring to a boil and boil for 30 minutes. Cool.

COPENHAGEN II

Rich pastry or cooky dough
  (recipe above)
8 eggs
1¼ cups sugar
2¼ cups blanched almonds,
  finely chopped

¾ cup flour
10 sheets phyllo pastry
Melted butter for pastry sheets
Syrup (below)

Line a 10×14×2-inch pan with pastry and bake in a 425-degree oven until lightly browned. Cool.

Beat eggs and sugar in an electric beater at high speed for 15 minutes or until pale in color and very thick and a spoonful takes some time to level out when poured back into the mixture. Combine almonds and flour and slowly fold into egg mixture by hand. Blend but do not beat. Turn mixture into baked pastry crust and top with phyllo sheets, brushing each with melted butter before putting on top of the egg mixture. Work quickly so the cake filling does not lose the air beaten into it. With a sharp knife pierce phyllo sheets every 2 inches. Bake in a preheated 400-degree oven for 45 minutes to 1 hour or until a toothpick inserted into the filling comes out clean. Cool. Cut into diamond or triangular serving pieces and pour the hot syrup over the cool cake. *30 servings*

Syrup:

In a saucepan combine 3½ cups water, 3 cups sugar, a cinnamon stick, several whole cloves, several slices of orange and lemon, and 1 teaspoon lemon juice. Bring to a boil and simmer for 20 to 30 minutes. Strain.

COPENHAGEN III

1 pound phyllo pastry sheets
1 pound sweet butter, melted
8 eggs, separated
1 cup sugar

1 tablespoon flour
1 teaspoon baking powder
1 pound almond paste
Syrup (below)

Butter a 12×16-inch pan and line with 8 to 10 sheets of phyllo pastry, brushing each sheet generously with melted butter before putting it in pan. Keep remaining pastry sheets covered with a damp towel while making filling.

Beat egg yolks with sugar until mixture is thick and pale in color. Fold in flour and baking powder. In a separate bowl break up almond paste as finely as possible; this will still be lumpy. Add egg yolk mixture and beat until fairly smooth. Beat egg whites until stiff but not dry and fold into egg yolk mixture. Fold in ⅛ cup of the melted butter. Pour filling into lined pan and cover with 6 to 8 sheets of phyllo, carefully buttering each layer. With a sharp pointed knife, carefully cut top layers of phyllo into squares. Bake in a 325-degree oven for 1 hour or until golden brown. Remove from oven and pour cool syrup over the hot cake. *Yield: 48 pieces*

Syrup:

In a saucepan combine 3 cups sugar, 1½ cups water, juice of ½ lemon, and 1 strip lemon peel. Bring to a boil and boil for 10 minutes. Strain and cool.

TRIGONA I

¾ *pound blanched almonds, ground*
¾ *pound walnut meats, ground*
1 *cup sugar*
3 *egg yolks*
1 *jigger brandy or whiskey*
1½ *teaspoons vanilla*
2 *teaspoons cream or evaporated milk*
1 *pound phyllo pastry sheets*
2 *cups (1 pound) sweet butter, melted*
Syrup (below)

Mix nuts and sugar. Beat egg yolks and add whiskey, vanilla, and cream or evaporated milk. Stir in nut mixture and blend well. Make balls the size of walnuts. If not moist enough to shape into little balls, add more cream. Cut sheets of phyllo pastry into thirds. Cover two thirds with waxed paper and a slightly dampened towel. From remaining third take one sheet at a time, spread evenly with melted butter, and fold into thirds lengthwise. Place a ball of nut mixture in lower corner. Fold and refold in triangle shape. Butter the triangle and place in a buttered pan or on a cooky sheet about ½ inch apart. Bake in a 350-degree oven for 15 to 20 minutes or until golden. Remove from oven and let stand for about 2 minutes. Then prick each of the *trigona* with a two-pronged fork and dip into the cool syrup. *Yield: 75 pieces*

Syrup:

1 cup water	¼ cup honey
1½ cups sugar	½ lemon, juice of

Combine all ingredients, bring to a boil, and boil for 10 minutes. Cool.

TRIGONA II

3 cups blanched almonds, ground	A few drops lemon juice
	Phyllo pastry sheets
2 cups sugar	Sweet butter, melted for brushing phyllo
2 cups water	
3 tablespoons rose water or 1 tablespoon vanilla	Confectioners' sugar

Mix together almonds, sugar, water, rose water or vanilla, and lemon juice. Cook over a low flame, stirring constantly, until mixture becomes thick and pasty. Cut phyllo pastry sheets as instructed in recipe above. Brush with butter and fold as above. Place 1 tablespoon of the almond mixture in corner of pastry and fold into triangle shape. Butter triangles and bake in a 350-degree oven for 30 minutes or until lightly browned. When slightly cool, sprinkle generously with confectioners' sugar. *36 servings*

BAKLAVA I

1 pound phyllo pastry sheets	5 tablespoons sugar
1½ cups (¾ pound) sweet butter, melted	1 teaspoon cinnamon
	Dash of clove
1 pound walnut meats, finely chopped	Syrup (below)

Place sheets of phyllo pastry in a 13×9×2-inch pan, brushing each second sheet evenly with butter. When 10 or 12 sheets are in place, combine walnuts, sugar, cinnamon, and clove, and spread one third of this mixture over the top sheet. Place another 5 or 6 buttered sheets of phyllo on top of nut mixture, sprinkle with another third of the nut mixture, and repeat with buttered phyllo sheets and the final third of the nut mixture. Spread remaining phyllo sheets on top, carefully buttering each second sheet. With a sharp knife cut *baklava* into diamond-shaped pieces. Heat remaining butter (there should be ½ cup) until very hot and beginning to brown, and pour evenly over the *baklava*. Sprinkle top with a few drops of cold water and bake in a 350-degree oven for 30 minutes. Reduce temperature to 300 degrees and continue to bake for 1 hour longer. Cool and pour hot syrup over the *baklava*. *30–36 servings*

Syrup:

In a saucepan combine 3½ cups water, 3 cups sugar, 1 teaspoon lemon juice, several slices orange and lemon, a cinnamon stick, and a few whole cloves. Bring to a boil and simmer for 20 minutes. Strain.

BAKLAVA II

1 pound blanched almonds, finely chopped	1 pound phyllo pastry sheets
1 cup sugar	2 cups (1 pound) sweet butter, melted
1 tablespoon cinnamon	Syrup (below)

Combine almonds, sugar, and cinnamon. Place 8 sheets of phyllo pastry, one at a time, in bottom of an 8×14×2-inch pan, brushing each sheet with melted butter. Sprinkle top sheet generously with some of the nut mixture and place 2 buttered phyllo sheets on top. Sprinkle with nut mixture. Continue adding buttered phyllo sheets, sprinkling every second sheet with nut mixture until all nut mixture is used. Place remaining phyllo sheets on top, buttering each sheet before placing in the pan. With a sharp knife cut *baklava* into small diamond-shaped pieces. Place a pan of water on the lowest shelf in a preheated 300-degree oven. Bake *baklava* on middle shelf of oven for 3 hours, making sure that the water pan is always full. Remove from oven and pour cool syrup over pastry. *30–36 servings*

Syrup:

In a saucepan combine ¾ cup sugar, ¾ cup honey, 2 cups water, juice of ½ lemon, and the squeezed lemon rind. Bring to a boil and boil for 20 minutes. Remove lemon rind and cool.

BAKLAVA III

3 pounds walnuts in shells	1 pound phyllo pastry sheets
1 cup sugar	1 pound butter, melted
1½ teaspoons cinnamon	Syrup (below)

Shell walnuts and finely chop the meat. Add sugar and cinnamon and mix well. Butter a large baking pan and line with 5 sheets of phyllo pastry, buttering each sheet evenly. Spread some of the nut mixture over entire surface. Add 2 buttered pastry sheets and spread evenly with nut mixture. Continue until all nut mixture is used, saving 5 sheets of phyllo for the top layer. Be sure to carefully butter each sheet of pastry. With a sharp knife cut *baklava* into diamond-shaped pieces. Bake in a 325-degree oven for 30 minutes, placing pan on middle shelf of oven. Move to top shelf and bake for an additional 30 minutes. Remove from oven and pour the hot syrup over the hot *baklava*. *30–36 servings*

Syrup:

In a saucepan combine 3 cups sugar and 2½ cups water. Bring to a boil and simmer for 15 minutes.

BAKLAVA WITH COOKY FILLING *Baklava me Yemisis Kourabieh*

1 pound toasted blanched almonds, or walnut meats or half of each, finely chopped	Dash of cinnamon
	1 pound phyllo pastry sheets
½ cup zwieback crumbs	1½ cups sweet butter, melted
4 tablespoons sugar	Cooky filling (below)
	Syrup (below)

Mix almonds or walnuts, or a combination of the two, with zwieback, sugar, and cinnamon. Brush 2 sheets of phyllo pastry evenly with butter and sprinkle with nut mixture. Place 2 buttered sheets of phyllo on top and sprinkle with nut mixture. Shape a portion of cooky filling into a ½-inch-thick roll and place the roll along one edge of the pastry sheets. Roll up loosely, cut into 2-inch slices, and place slices in a buttered cake pan. (Continue in this method until all phyllo pastry and/or cooky filling is used.) Brush tops of each slice with butter and bake in a 350-degree oven for 20 minutes or until lightly browned. Dip the hot *baklava* slices, one at a time, in cold syrup, allowing each piece to remain in the syrup for a few minutes. *36 servings*

Cooky Filling:

Cream 2 cups sweet butter until light. Gradually beat in 1 cup confectioners' sugar and continue to beat until mixture is fluffy. Add 1 egg yolk and ½ tablespoon vanilla or almond extract and blend well. Work in about 4 cups flour to made a medium-soft dough.

Syrup:

In a saucepan combine 4 cups sugar and 4 cups water. Bring to a boil and boil for 15 minutes or until syrup is slightly thick. Add 1 cup honey and again bring to the boiling point. Add lemon juice to taste, and cool.

ROLLED BAKLAVA *Baklava Orthi*

2 pounds phyllo pastry sheets
1½ pounds sweet butter, melted
4 pounds walnut meats, finely
  chopped

4 tablespoons sugar
3 teaspoons cinnamon
½ teaspoon clove
Syrup (below)

Take 4 sheets of phyllo pastry, keeping remaining sheets covered with a damp towel. Brush each sheet with melted butter and lay one on top of the other. Mix walnuts, sugar, cinnamon, and clove. Sprinkle some of the mixture evenly over the top buttered sheet and roll up tightly like a jelly roll. Cut roll into 2-inch pieces and set the pieces upright in a large buttered pan. Continue, using another 4 buttered sheets of phyllo, sprinkling with nut mixture, rolling, and cutting, until the pan or pans are full and all the nut mixture is used. Spoon about 1 teaspoon melted butter over each piece and bake in a 350-degree oven for 10 minutes. Turn over each piece, setting it upright again, spoon another teaspoon melted butter over each piece, and continue baking for 20 to 30 minutes or until golden brown. Remove from oven and dip each piece into cold thick syrup. Drain on cake racks. *48 servings*

Syrup:

In a saucepan combine 4 cups sugar, 2 cups water, juice of ½ lemon, and 1 small jar honey. Bring to a boil and simmer for 30 minutes, removing scum as it rises to the surface.

GLACE BAKLAVA *Baklava Glasé*

4 eggs
1 pound blanched almonds,
  finely chopped
1½ cups sugar
1 pound mixed glacé fruit,
  finely chopped

1½ cups sugar
1 pound phyllo pastry sheets
1 pound sweet butter, melted
Syrup (below)

Beat eggs until light. Fold in almonds and sugar. Stir in fruit.

Take 2 sheets of phyllo pastry, brush one at a time with melted butter, and place one on top of the other. On the long end of the phyllo sheet spread some of the fruit-and-nut mixture in a band about 1 inch wide. Fold in ends and roll like a jelly roll. Place on a cooky sheet and brush top with melted butter. Make diagonal slits along the whole length, about 1½ inches apart, being careful not to cut all the way through. Continue making the rolls until all nut mixture is used. Bake in a preheated 350-degree oven for about 1½ hours or until golden brown. Cut pieces through entire roll. Dip hot *baklava* pieces in cold syrup and drain well. *48 servings*

Syrup:

3 *cups sugar*	½ *lemon, juice of*
2 *cups water*	1 *stick cinnamon*

In a saucepan combine all ingredients. Bring to a boil and boil for 20 minutes. Cool.

SARAGLI

1½ *pounds walnut meats or half*	½ *cup sugar*
walnuts and half blanched	2 *pounds phyllo pastry sheets*
almonds, chopped	1 *pound sweet butter, melted*
3 *teaspoons cinnamon*	*Syrup (below)*
1 *teaspoon clove*	

Combine nuts, cinnamon, clove, and sugar. Take 1 sheet of phyllo pastry, keeping remaining sheets covered with a damp towel. Brush the sheet with melted butter and cut in half. Spoon some of the walnut mixture across one edge and fold ends over to keep mixture in. Place a ¼-inch round dowel, 12 inches long, across mixture and roll up tightly like a jelly roll. It will look like a narrow cylinder. Push both ends toward center so it shirrs, slide dowel out, and carefully place the *saragli* in an ungreased pan. Continue in this manner, rolling and shirring, tightly packing as many *saragli* as the pan will hold. Brush with melted butter. Bake in a preheated 350-degree oven for 30 to 40 minutes or until golden brown. Cut into 2-inch-long serving pieces and, while still hot from the oven, dip each piece into cold syrup. Drain on wire cake racks. *48 servings*

Syrup:

In a saucepan combine 4 cups sugar, 2 cups water, juice of ½ lemon, 1 small jar honey, and 1 stick cinnamon. Bring to a boil and simmer for 30 minutes, removing scum as it rises to surface.

GALATOBOUREKO I

8 egg yolks
8 tablespoons sugar
1½ quarts warm milk
6 tablespoons cornstarch
1 cup heavy cream

1 tablespoon vanilla
½ pound phyllo pastry sheets
1 cup sweet butter, melted
Syrup (below)

Beat egg yolks and sugar until mixture is thick and pale in color. Stir in warm milk alternately with the cornstarch and cook over low heat, stirring constantly, until mixture almost reaches a boil. Remove from heat and stir in heavy cream and vanilla.

Place half the sheets of phyllo pastry in a well-buttered 9×13-inch pan, buttering each sheet generously before putting in the pan. Pour cream mixture into pan and top with remaining sheets of phyllo, buttering each evenly. With a sharp knife cut top pastry into 4 or 5 strips. Bake in a preheated 375-degree oven for 45 to 50 minutes or until golden. Remove from oven and pour cool syrup over the hot *galatoboureko*. Do not cover pan or it will make the cake soggy. Cool and cut into squares before serving. *24 servings*

Syrup:

Combine 3½ cups sugar, 2½ cups boiling water, and 1 teaspoon lemon juice. Bring to a boil and simmer for 15 minutes. Cool.

GALATOBOUREKO II

2 quarts milk
12 eggs, lightly beaten
1 cup regular farina
1 cup sugar
4 tablespoons butter

1 teaspoon vanilla
1 pound phyllo pastry sheets
1 pound sweet butter, melted
Syrup (below)

In a saucepan combine milk, eggs, farina, sugar, and the 4 tablespoons butter. Cook over low heat, stirring constantly, until mixture is very hot and thickens. Remove from heat and stir in vanilla.

Place 10 sheets of phyllo pastry in a 12×16-inch baking pan, buttering each sheet evenly before placing it in the pan. Pour filling into pan and cover with 10 more sheets of phyllo, again brushing each sheet generously with butter. With a sharp knife cut top pastry into diamond-shaped pieces and bake in a 400-degree oven for 50 minutes to 1 hour or until golden brown. Remove from oven and pour cool syrup over the hot *galatoboureko*. Cool in pan, letting the syrup be absorbed. *36–48 servings*

Syrup:

In a saucepan combine 3 cups sugar, 2 cups water, and 1 slice lemon. Bring to a boil and boil for 15 minutes. Cool.

GALATOBOUREKO III

1 quart milk
1 cup cream of rice
1 cup sugar
Pinch of salt

4 eggs, separated
1 cup butter, melted
10 phyllo pastry sheets
Syrup (below)

Scald milk. Add cream of rice, sugar, and salt and cook, stirring constantly, until mixture is thickened. Cool slightly. Add egg yolks to the rice mixture and stir well. Cook over low heat, stirring constantly, for 2 minutes. Cool. Fold in stiffly beaten egg whites.

Butter 5 sheets of phyllo pastry and place, one on top of another, in a 10×14×2-inch pan. Add cooled rice mixture and cover with 5 more buttered sheets of phyllo pastry. With a sharp knife cut top layer of pastry sheets into diagonal pieces, leaving a border of 2 inches uncut. Bake in a 350-degree oven for 1 hour until golden brown. Pour cold syrup over the hot cake, or cool cake and pour hot syrup over. *30 servings*

Syrup:

1½ cups sugar
2 cups water
¼-lemon wedge

Combine ingredients, bring to a boil, and boil for 15 minutes.

CUSTARD HORNS *Floyeres*

6 egg yolks
1 cup sugar
1 cup farina
6 cups scalded milk

Lemon peel or vanilla
10–12 phyllo pastry sheets
1 cup butter, melted
Syrup (below)

Beat egg yolks with sugar. Add farina and mix well. Slowly stir in scalded milk and lemon peel or vanilla. Cook, stirring constantly, until mixture thickens, about 15 minutes. Cool.

Cut sheets of phyllo pastry in half. Keep pastry not in use carefully covered with a lightly dampened towel. Butter each piece evenly and fold in half. Place 1 tablespoon of the rice mixture at one end and fold ends toward middle. Butter and roll up each piece. Place in a buttered pan and butter tops. Bake in a 350-degree oven for 25 to 30 minutes or until golden brown. Prick *floyeres* carefully with a fork and pour the cool syrup over them. *20–24 servings*

Syrup:

4 cups sugar
2 cups water
1 lemon, juice of

Combine ingredients, bring to a boil, and boil for 15 minutes. Cool.

KADAIFE

1 pound kadaife pastry*
1½ cups walnut meats, finely chopped
¾ cup blanched almonds, finely chopped

¼ cup sugar
1 teaspoon cinnamon
1 cup butter, melted
1 cup hot milk
Syrup (below)

Arrange half the *kadaife* pastry in a greased 9×9×2-inch pan. Combine walnuts, almonds, sugar, and cinnamon and sprinkle over the *kadaife* in the pan. Pour half the melted butter over the nut mixture and top with remaining *kadaife*. Pour hot milk and remaining butter over top *kadaife*. Cover and bake in a 350-degree oven for 35 minutes. Remove from oven and immediately pour hot syrup over pastry. Cover with a towel and with another pan and let stand until cool. Cut into 2-inch squares. *20 servings*

Syrup:

Combine ¾ cup honey, ¼ cup sugar, and 1 cup water. Bring to a boil and boil for 5 minutes.

KADAIFE EKMEK

*2 pounds kadaife pastry**	*Syrup (below)*
1½ pounds sweet butter, melted	*6 tablespoons cornstarch*
1 cup warm milk	*2 quarts heavy cream*

Spread the *kadaife* on tablecloth to dry for 1 hour. Place the *kadaife* in two 8×11-inch pans. Pour half the melted butter over the pastry in each pan and bake in a 350-degree oven for 20 minutes or until pastry is a pale rosy color. Remove from oven and sprinkle the pastry in each pan with warm milk. Pour half the syrup over the pastry in each pan, cover pans with a towel to keep pastry moist, and let cool.

Make a thin paste of the cornstarch and a little of the cream. Heat remaining cream to almost boiling, stir in cornstarch mixture, and cook, stirring constantly, until cream is thick and no longer tastes of starch. Cool and chill. Spread filling over the pastry in one pan. Invert pastry from the other pan on top. Cut into squares and turn pieces upside down on serving dish. *20 servings*

Syrup:

In a sauce pan combine 3 cups sugar, 2 cups water, and juice of ½ lemon. Bring to a boil and boil for 15 minutes. Cool.

PUDDINGS

CARAMEL CUSTARD *Krema Karamela*

1½ cups sugar	2 teaspoons vanilla
1 quart milk	½ cup blanched almonds,
6 eggs	slivered (optional)
¼ teaspoon salt	

Caramelize 1 cup sugar in a heavy skillet over low heat, stirring constantly, until golden. Don't let it get too dark or it will become bitter. Pour into a mold, plain or fancy, coating all sides. Mold should be warm to prevent syrup from cracking.

Scald milk and cool slightly. Beat eggs, add remaining ½ cup sugar, salt, and vanilla, and beat well. Slowly stir in milk. Strain mixture into coated mold. Place mold in a pan containing 1 inch hot water and bake in a 325-degree oven for about 1 to 1½ hours or until a knife inserted in center comes out clean. Remove from oven, cool, and refrigerate at least a few hours before serving. Invert on a chilled platter and unmold, spooning syrup over the custard. If desired, sprinkle almonds on top. *8–10 servings*

RICE PUDDING *Rizogalo*

½ cup rice	1 cup sugar
½ quart water	1 teaspoon salt
1 quart milk	Cinnamon
4 egg yolks	

Simmer rice in water and milk for about 45 minutes or until sauce is thick and rice is soft. Beat egg yolks and sugar until thick and pale in color. Gradually stir in rice pudding, mix well, and return to saucepan. Add salt and cook over low heat for about 2 minutes, stirring constantly to prevent curdling. Pour into pudding dishes and sprinkle with cinnamon. *8 servings*

EASY RICE PUDDING *Rizogalo*

1 quart milk	1 teaspoon vanilla
½ cup rice	½ cup cream or evaporated milk
½ cup sugar	Nutmeg or cinnamon
½ teaspoon salt	

Slowly heat milk. Add rice, sugar, and salt and cook over low heat for 45 minutes, stirring occasionally. Add vanilla and cream or evaporated milk. Cool. Sprinkle with nutmeg or cinnamon to taste. *6 servings*

VARIATION: ½ cup raisins or a little grated lemon rind may be added.

HALVAH

2½ cups sugar	½ cup unblanched almonds, split
3 cups water	lengthwise
1 cup sweet butter	Cinnamon
1 box (14-ounces) regular farina	

In saucepan combine sugar and water. Bring to a boil and boil for 10 minutes. Set syrup aside. In another saucepan melt butter without letting it brown. Stir in farina and continue to stir over very low heat for 45 minutes, being careful that it does not brown. The mixture should be kept as light as possible. Add almonds and slowly stir in syrup. Continue to cook, stirring, until mixture holds its shape. Pour into a mold and cool. Unmold and sprinkle generously with cinnamon. *20 servings*

HALVAH POLITIKO

¼ pound (1 stick) butter	1 cup milk
1 cup regular farina	1 cup water
½ cup pignolia nuts (optional)	Cinnamon
1 cup sugar	

In a heavy frying pan melt butter. Stir in farina and nuts, if desired, and brown over low heat for about 15 minutes, stirring constantly. In a saucepan combine sugar, milk, and water. Bring to a boil and boil for 10 minutes. When farina is browned, slowly stir in the hot syrup. Turn off heat, cover skillet with a dish towel to absorb steam, cover with lid, and let stand for 30 minutes. Serve in bowls, sprinkled with cinnamon. Or pour the halvah onto a shallow platter to cool. Cut into diamond-shaped pieces and serve sprinkled with cinnamon. *12 servings*

HALVAH TOU KOUTALIOU

2½ cups flour
2 tablespoons regular farina
1 cup oil
2 cups water

1 cup sugar
Cinnamon
Walnuts, chopped

In a heavy skillet brown flour and farina in the oil. In a saucepan combine water and sugar, bring to a boil, and boil for 10 minutes. When flour mixture is brown, gradually stir in the syrup and cook, stirring, until mixture is thick and all the syrup is absorbed. Remove from heat and cover with a dish towel to absorb the steam. When slightly cooled, mold in a tablespoon and carefully unmold onto a plate. Sprinkle with cinnamon and chopped walnuts. *20 servings.*

FRIED CAKES

HONEY ROLLS I   *Diples I*

3 eggs, separated
1 teaspoon baking powder
About 1½–2 cups flour, sifted

Hot oil for frying
Syrup (below)
Cinnamon

Beat egg whites with baking powder until stiff. Beat egg yolks lightly, add to egg whites, and beat until creamy. Stir in enough flour to make a soft dough. Turn out dough on lightly floured board and knead with oiled hands until smooth. Dough will be a little sticky. Keep kneading until dough blisters and forms bubbles when sliced with a knife. Form dough into 1-inch balls. Roll out each ball very thinly and cut into rectangles. Drop, one at a time, into hot fat (360 degrees), turn immediately, using two forks, and roll up into a cylinder. Remove from fat when golden. Dip immediately into hot syrup. Place on cake racks to drain and sprinkle with cinnamon. *Yield: approximately 5 dozen*

Syrup:

In saucepan combine 1 cup honey, 2 cups sugar, and 1 cup water. Bring to a boil and boil for 10 to 15 minutes.

HONEY ROLLS II *Diples II*

6 medium eggs
½ teaspoon baking powder
¼ teaspoon salt
3½ cups flour, sifted
About ½ cup olive oil

Shortening for frying
Honey
Cinnamon and/or pistachio
    nuts, chopped

In an electric beater beat eggs until light. Sift together baking powder, salt, and flour. Gradually add to eggs, beating constantly. When mixture reaches the point where it is too stiff to beat further, work in remaining flour by hand.

Turn dough onto an unfloured board, add olive oil, one tablespoon at a time, and work in with the hands until dough is smooth. This takes about 10 minutes. Then take a quarter of the dough at a time and roll out paper-thin on a heavily floured board. Cut into 4×6-inch strips. Drop strips, one at a time, into hot fat (360 degrees), turn immediately, using two forks, then roll up quickly while still in the fat as you would a piece of paper. Fry until golden but not browned. Drain on absorbent paper. To serve honey rolls in the traditional manner, dribble honey over them, then sprinkle with cinnamon and/or nuts. *This recipe makes about 45 rolls.* They will keep for months in a covered jar or tin. *Yield: approximately 4–5 dozen*

SWEET FRITTERS I *Loukoumades I*

1 package yeast
3 cups lukewarm water
1 cup warm milk
1 tablespoon salt
2 eggs, beaten

Flour as needed
Oil or shortening for frying
Syrup (below)
Cinnamon

Soften yeast in a little of the warm water. Combine remaining water and milk. Stir in yeast, salt, and beaten eggs. Beat in enough flour to make a thick, sticky batter. Put batter in a warm place for a few hours, or overnight, to rise. Stir batter down and mix well. Drop from a tablespoon into hot deep cooking oil (360 degrees) and fry until brown on all sides. Remove from oil, drain on absorbent paper, then dip into hot syrup. Place on racks to drain and sprinkle with cinnamon. *Yield: approximately 4 dozen*

Syrup:

In a saucepan combine 1 cup honey, 1 cup water, and 2 cups sugar. Bring to a boil and boil for 10 to 15 minutes.

SWEET FRITTERS II *Loukoumades II*

1 package yeast
1 cup rice water
1 cup yogurt
½ cup water
¼ teaspoon baking powder

Flour as needed
Oil or shortening for frying
Syrup (recipe above)
Cinnamon

Soften yeast in ¼ cup of the rice water. Stir in remaining rice water, yogurt, water, and baking powder. Stir in enough flour to make a soft, sticky batter. Put batter in a warm place for a few hours, or overnight, to rise. Stir batter down and mix well. Drop from a tablespoon into hot deep fat (360 degrees) and fry until browned on all sides. Remove from fat, drain on absorbent paper, then dip into hot syrup. Place on racks to drain and sprinkle with cinnamon. *Yield: approximately 4 dozen*

SWEET FRITTERS III *Loukoumades III*

1 cup milk
1¼ cups self-rising cake flour
Oil for frying

Honey
Chopped nuts
Cinnamon

Combine milk and flour and beat until batter is thick and bubbly. In a heavy saucepan heat 2 inches of oil to 360 degrees. Drop batter by the tablespoonful into the hot oil. Fry only a few at a time and turn as soon as the *loukoumades* are golden brown on the underside. When brown all over, drain on absorbent paper, place on serving platter, and sprinkle with honey, chopped nuts, and cinnamon. Serve warm. *Yield: approximately 2–2½ dozen*

SWEET FRITTERS IV *Loukoumades IV*

1 stick (½ cup) butter
1 cup water
1 cup flour
1 teaspoon baking powder
2 tablespoons sugar

4 eggs
1 egg white, stiffly beaten
Oil or shortening for frying
Syrup (below)
Cinnamon

Heat butter and water in a saucepan until butter melts and mixture comes to a boil. Sift together flour, baking powder, and sugar. Add dry ingredients all at once to the boiling butter-water mixture and stir vigorously over low heat until mixture forms a ball in the center of the pan. Remove from heat and cool for 5 minutes. Then beat in eggs one egg at a time and beat after each addition until batter is smooth and glossy. Fold in beaten egg white. Drop batter by tablespoonfuls into hot oil (375 degrees) and fry until golden on all sides. Drain on absorbent paper. Pour syrup over the *loukoumades* and sprinkle with cinnamon. *Yield: approximately 3–4 dozen*

Syrup:

In a saucepan combine 2 cups sugar, 1½ cups water, a strip of lemon peel, and 1 stick cinnamon. Bring to a boil and boil for 15 minutes. Remove from heat and stir in ¾ cup honey.

MISCELLANEOUS

MISCELLANEOUS

A few special Greek dishes, which do not fit into the other chapters in this book, are included here. Among them are basic recipes for Greek bread and Greek coffee, recipes for making your own yogurt from milk and a few tablespoons of commercial yogurt, and several recipes for some of the sweet preserves for which the Greeks are noted.

For centuries the Greeks have preserved all kinds of vegetables, fruits, and flower petals, originally in honey and later in a sugar syrup. These they serve for dessert, with their afternoon coffee, or at the breakfast table. The fragrant ROSE PETAL JELLY, which never fails to intrigue the tourist in Greece, is made on the island of Chios for export to America, but those of you with a garden full of sweet-smelling roses might like to try your own.

GREEK BREAD *Psomi*

1 cup hot milk	1 envelope yeast
¼ cup shortening	¼ cup warm water
1 teaspoon salt	4 cups sifted flour
2 tablespoons sugar	Melted butter

Heat milk and stir in shortening, salt, and sugar. Soften yeast in warm water. Sift flour into bowl. Make a well in the flour and pour the softened yeast into the well. Gradually stir in warm milk mixture to make a firm dough. Knead dough until smooth. Put dough into a greased bowl and let rise for 1½ hours in a warm place. Knead again and let rise again for 1½ hours. Knead and form into loaves. Place loaves in greased, floured bread pans, brush tops with melted butter, and let rise in a warm place for about 1 hour or until double in bulk. Bake in a 375-degree oven for about 45 minutes or until loaves are golden. *Yield: 2 loaves*

EGGS AND CHICKEN LIVERS *Sikotakia me Avga*

 2 *chicken livers*   *Salt and pepper*
 6 *tablespoons butter*   *4 eggs, well beaten*
 1 *onion, finely chopped*

Cut livers into small pieces. In a skillet heat 4 tablespoons of the butter and in it sauté onion until tender and lightly browned. Add chicken livers, season to taste, and brown lightly. Melt remaining butter in the same skillet. Add eggs and cook over low heat, stirring constantly, until eggs are set but still creamy. Turn onto serving platter and serve. *2–3 servings*

EGGS WITH TOMATOES AND ONIONS
Avga me Domates ke Kremidia

 2 *tomatoes, peeled and chopped*   *4 eggs*
 1 *onion, chopped*   *Salt and pepper*
 3 *tablespoons butter*

In a skillet sauté tomatoes and onion in 2 tablespoons of the butter over low heat until excess moisture is evaporated and onion is tender. Beat eggs and season to taste with salt and pepper. In another skillet heat remaining butter. Add eggs and cook, stirring, over low heat until eggs begin to set. Pour tomato-onion mixture on top and continue to cook, stirring slightly, until eggs are set. *2–3 servings*

YOGURT I *Yiaourti*

 3 *quarts milk*
 1 *cup heavy cream*
 5 *tablespoons yogurt*

Bring milk and cream to a boil, stirring so the mixture does not stick to bottom of saucepan. Cook for about 10 minutes. Remove from heat and allow to cool until your little finger can remain in the milk for about 20 seconds. Thin the yogurt in a cup with a little of the milk and add to the remainder of the milk. Stir until well blended. Pour into a large heavy bowl or into individual molds. Cover well and keep in a warm place for 6 to 8 hours or overnight until yogurt is set. Refrigerate and serve. If thicker yogurt is preferred, empty the yogurt into a muslin bag and suspend to allow excess liquid to drain out.

Yogurt may be served as a sauce over vegetables or rice, or as desired. *Yield: 24 cups*

YOGURT II *Yiaourti*

1 quart milk
1 small can evaporated milk
2 tablespoons yogurt

Bring milk to a boil and simmer for 20 minutes, stirring occasionally. Add evaporated milk and stir well. Allow to cool until just luke-warm. In a cup mix yogurt with ½ cup of the cooled milk. Blend well and stir into milk. Blend again. Pour into thick glasses or cups and keep in a warm place covered with a dish towel for several hours until thick. Serve cold. *Yield: 8–9 cups*

KOLYVA

2 pounds whole wheat	4 cups walnuts, finely chopped
Water to cover	¼ cup parsley, chopped
1 teaspoon salt	(optional)
4 cups flour	1 pound confectioners' sugar
1 cup white raisins	White Jordan almonds
2 tablespoons cumin	Blanched almonds
2 tablespoons cinnamon	Silver dragées
½–1 cup sugar	

Wash wheat with warm water. Place in a saucepan, add water to cover generously and salt, and simmer until wheat is soft. Drain in colander. Spread on linen towel and allow wheat to dry thoroughly. Put flour in a heavy skillet and cook over very low heat, stirring constantly, until golden. Be careful not to scorch it. Mix wheat with half the flour and add raisins, cumin, cinnamon, and sugar. Blend well. Place mixture on a tray, spreading evenly. Spread chopped walnuts and parsley over mixture. Then spread remaining flour evenly over entire tray. Sift confectioners' sugar over top and carefully press sugar down firmly with waxed paper or spatula.

Decorate tray of *kolyva* with Jordan almonds, blanched almonds, and silver *dragées*. Usually a large cross made of silver *dragées* is placed in the center of the *kolyva* and the initials of the deceased are formed with white almonds on each side. Further designs on border and corners are made with remaining almonds and *dragées* as desired.

VARVARA

½ *pound wheat, boiled*	1½ *cups flour*
3 *quarts water*	*Cinnamon*
1 *cup raisins*	*Chopped nuts*
1 *cup sugar*	*Pomegranate seeds (optional)*

Add boiled wheat to water, bring to a boil, and boil until wheat puffs up. Water should not be absorbed. Add raisins and sugar. Brown flour in roasting pan in oven, stirring occasionally. When flour is golden, add to boiled wheat mixture, stirring well to moisten flour. Shut off heat and let mixture stand. Serve with cinnamon, nuts, and pomegranate seeds if desired. If mixture becomes too thick, stir in a little water. *Varvara* is eaten cold.

GREEK COFFEE *Kafes*

These ingredients are given for 1 demitasse cup. Increase the measurements for the number of cups you wish to serve. Sugar is added to the coffee while it is cooked; therefore more or less sugar may be added according to taste.

1 *tablespoon Greek or Turkish*
  coffee
½ *teaspoon sugar*
1 *demitasse water*

Place the coffee and sugar in a Greek or Turkish coffeepot (*kafeïbriki*) and blend. Add the water and stir until well mixed. Place on heat and wait until coffee comes to a boil, stirring occasionally to be certain all the coffee, sugar, and water are mixed. As soon as the coffee has come to a boil and reaches the rim of the coffeepot, remove pot from heat and pour a little coffee into each demitasse to be served. This is very important, as the first boil forms the *kaïmak*, or cream of the coffee. Return the pot to the heat and allow coffee to boil to the rim again. Pour a little coffee into each cup, being very careful not to disturb the *kaïmak* in each cup. Repeat this procedure once again. Serve the coffee hot. Since the grounds are served in the cup with the coffee, the Greek guest allows his coffee to stand for a few seconds before sipping. This allows the grounds to settle to the bottom of the cup. The coffee is carefully sipped without disturbing the grounds.

Note: If preferred, coffee and sugar may be stirred into boiling water. Proceed as above.

EASTER EGGS *Paskalina Avga*

Greek Easter eggs are always dyed a deep crimson. For the best results use an imported red dye. One package of dye will color 18 eggs.

Dilute the powder in ½ cup white vinegar. Add this mixture to sufficient warm water to cover the eggs. Bring water to a boil and simmer, stirring occasionally, for about 5 minutes. Remove pot from heat and add eggs. The eggs should be at room temperature or they are apt to crack. Return to heat and simmer eggs for 15 minutes. Remove eggs, cool slightly, then rub each egg with an oiled cloth.

FASKOMILO TEA

> *1 teaspoon* faskomilo (*sage*)
> *Sugar to taste*
> *1 cup boiling water*

Combine ingredients, bring to a boil, and boil for 5 minutes. Strain and serve hot.

CAMOMILE TEA *Hamomilo*

> *1 camomile tea bag*
> *Sugar to taste*
> *1 cup boiling water*

Combine ingredients, bring to a boil, and boil for 5 minutes. Strain and serve hot.

ROSE PETAL JELLY *Triantafillo Glyko*

> *1 pound rose petals*   *½ teaspoon sour salt or 1½*
> *2 pounds sugar*   *lemons, juice of*
> *1 cup water*

Only petals from very sweet-smelling roses may be used for jelly. Remove the white tip from each rose petal and carefully wash petals. Cover the bottom of a large saucepan with sugar, add a layer of rose petals, a layer of sugar, and so forth until all the rose petals and the sugar have been used. Add the water. If using sour salt dissolve in a little water and sprinkle over mixture. If sour salt is not available, add lemon juice. Bring to a boil, cover, and simmer until sugar forms a stiff ball when a little is dropped on a cold saucer. Remove from heat and cool. Pour into serving dishes or jars.

GRAPEFRUIT MARMALADE *Frapa Marmalada*

Grapefruit	Sugar
Water	¼ lemon, juice of

Remove pulp from grapefruit shell, slice rind into strips, then slice strips thinly. Place rind into saucepan and cover with water. Soak overnight. Bring to a boil and simmer until rind is transparent, adding more water if needed. Measure fruit and liquid, add equal amount of sugar, and simmer until the jelly stage is reached. Add lemon juice and simmer for another 5 minutes. Pour into sterilized jars and seal tightly.

LOUKOUMI *Turkish Delight*

3 tablespoons gelatin	Red or green food coloring
½ cup cold water	Pistachio nuts or toasted
2 cups sugar	almonds (optional)
½ cup hot water	Confectioners' sugar
1 orange, grated rind, juice of	

Soften gelatin in cold water. Combine sugar and hot water and heat to boiling. Add softened gelatin and simmer for 20 minutes. Add orange juice and rind and coloring. Strain into loaf pan. The pan should be large enough so that the mixture is from ½ to 1 inch deep. Add nuts if desired. Chill until firm. When cold turn onto a board, cut into cubes, and roll in confectioners' sugar.

GRATED QUINCE *Kythoni Xysto*

1 pound quince	2 sticks cinnamon or 1–2
2 cups sugar	geranium leaves
¾ cup water	½ lemon, juice of

Peel the quince and grate the flesh on a coarse grater. Put grated quince in saucepan with sugar, water, and flavoring. Simmer for about 1 hour or until syrup thickens to the consistency of honey. Add lemon juice at the end of cooking time to prevent syrup from crystallizing. Stir at intervals and skim off any scum that rises to top while cooking.

QUINCE PUREE   *Kythoni Pelté*

1 cup sugar
2 cups quince stock (recipe
below)

½ lemon, juice of

Blend sugar and quince stock and bring to a boil. Cook, stirring constantly, to the jellying point. Add lemon juice. Cool.

QUINCE FORMS   *Kythonopasto*

2–3 pounds quince
Water

Sugar
Bay leaves

Peel quince and slice in 2-inch pieces. Add water to cover, bring to a boil, and boil until fruit is tender. Drain and save water for making QUINCE PUREE (above). Press quince through a sieve to make a purée. Use 1 cup sugar to each cup of purée. Combine purée and sugar in a saucepan and add about ½ cup water. Bring to a boil and boil, stirring constantly, until mixture comes away from the sides of the pan. Cool. Shape as desired either in diamond-shaped forms, pear-shaped forms with a clove on the end, or apricot shapes. Place pieces of bay leaves under each quince form and allow to dry in a cool place for 1 to 2 days before storing. Roll each piece in sugar after it is thoroughly dry.

SOUR CHERRY PRESERVES   *Vissino Glyko*

1 pound black or red sour
cherries
2 cups sugar

½ cup water
½ lemon, juice of

Wash and pit cherries, but keep pits in a small bowl. Place cherries in a saucepan in layers and sprinkle each layer with sugar. Add water to the cherry pits, stir slightly, drain, and add this water to the cherries. Allow mixture to stand for 1 hour, then bring to a boil and simmer for 30 minutes or until syrup thickens to consistency of honey. Stir gently at intervals while cooking and skim off any scum that rises to top. Add lemon juice at end of cooking time to prevent syrup from crystallizing.

EGGPLANT PRESERVES   *Melitzanakia*

1 pound tiny eggplants	*3 cups sugar*
1 teaspoon powdered lime	*2½ cups water*
1 quart water	*Lemon wedge*
Water to cover	*Blanched almonds*

Pare eggplant. Dilute powdered lime in the 1 quart water and soak eggplant for 4 to 5 hours. Rinse well and drain on towels. Put into saucepan and add water to cover. Bring to a boil and boil for 1 hour. Drain again and dry thoroughly. Cut 2 or 3 slits in each eggplant.

In a saucepan combine sugar, the 2½ cups water, and wedge of lemon. Bring to a boil and boil until syrup spins a light thread. Cool. Drop eggplant into syrup. If some excess moisture from the eggplant dilutes the syrup, reboil to thicken. When cool, remove eggplants and stuff slits with blanched almonds.

WATERMELON RIND PRESERVES   *Karpouzi Glyko*

1 pound watermelon rind	*2 sticks cinnamon*
1½ cups sugar	*½ cup toasted blanched almonds*
½ cup honey	*½ lemon, juice of*
½ cup water	

Peel watermelon rind and cube. Put rind in a saucepan with sugar, honey, water, and cinnamon sticks. Bring to a boil and simmer for 1 hour. Stir at intervals and skim off any scum that rises to top while cooking. Add almonds and lemon juice at end of cooking.

Note: Watermelon rind may be soaked for 4 to 5 hours in 1 teaspoon powdered lime diluted in 1 quart water. Rinse well several times before cooking.

TOMATO PRESERVES (Sweet)   *Domates Toursi Glykes*

Water	*5 pounds sugar*
10 pounds plum tomatoes	*5 cups water*
1 package liquid lime	*1 tablespoon lemon juice*

Bring a large pot of water to a boil. Add tomatoes, turn off heat, and let tomatoes steep in the boiling water for 2 to 3 minutes. Drain and cover immediately with cold water. Skin tomatoes and scoop out seeds. Cover tomatoes with cold water and add the package of liquid lime. Let tomatoes soak in the lime solution for 3 hours, then drain, wash tomatoes thoroughly, and spread on towels to drain. In a large kettle combine sugar and water. Bring to a boil and simmer until syrup thickens. Add tomatoes and continue to cook until syrup is thick. Add lemon juice, remove from heat, and let stand overnight. Next day bring syrup to a boil again and boil until thick. Pack in sterilized jars and seal immediately. Serve as a sweet relish.

Note: Liquid lime may be purchased at the drug store.

GLOSSARY

AHINI – sea urchins, served as appetizers. The roe is sprinkled with lemon juice and olive oil.

AMYGTHALA – almonds, much favored by the Greeks.

AMYGTHALOTA – a sweet cooky similar to marzipan, made of ground almonds and sugar, shaped in the form of little pears, and dipped in rose water.

ANDITHIA – endive, a vegetable used in salads, braised dishes, and stews.

ANGINARES – artichokes, a favorite vegetable of the Greeks. Care must be taken in preparing artichokes so that they do not darken. Frozen artichokes, defrosted, can be substituted in these recipes.

ANGINAROKARDOULES – artichoke hearts.

ANGOURIA – cucumbers, served in salads or as appetizers, either stuffed or plain.

ANITHO – fresh dill; excellent with avgolemono sauce.

ARNI, ARNAKI – lamb, the national dish of Greece. Lamb used by the Greeks is spring lamb or baby lamb. The Easter dinner features the milk-fed whole baby lamb, which, if possible, has been roasted on a spit.

ARNI TIS TIHIS – literally translated means "lamb of luck or fortune." As this lamb is cooked in foil or parchment paper, it might require good luck or good fortune to get a portion cooked to your taste. However, when you unwrap your portion and inhale the mouth-watering aroma, you will feel your luck is good indeed. *Klepthes*, or guerrillas, cooked their food in this manner, in the mountains of Greece, so that the aroma of their cooking would not reach the Turkish troops and thus give away their guerrilla camps.

ASPARANGI – asparagus.

ASTAKO – lobster.

ATZEM PILAF – the term used for a dish of meat or poultry, onions, and rice. Very good, especially for family dinners.

AVGA – eggs.

AVGOLEMONO – the favorite sauce of Greek cookery. It is used in soups, and stews and over meats and vegetables.

BAKALIAROS – codfish, usually salted codfish.

BAKLAVA – the most famous of Greek desserts. It is made with nuts, spices, butter, phyllo pastry, and syrup, and it is delectable.

BAMYES – okra. Okra should be trimmed carefully and soaked in vinegar and water. Frozen or canned okra may be substituted in these recipes, but a little vinegar should be added while cooking.

BARBOUNI – red mullet, a fish much favored by the Greeks. Barbouni may be fried or broiled.

BIZELIA – fresh green peas.

BOUREKIA, BOUREKAKIA – savory dishes made with phyllo pastry, either in a pie or in small rolls or triangles.

BULGUR – whole wheat grain, served in the same manner as rice.

CAPAMA – *see* KAPAMA.

CHRISTOPSOMO – the sweet bread baked at Christmas.

COPENHAGEN – an elegant dessert first made in honor of King George I, who was a prince of Denmark elected to the throne of Greece in 1863.

DIOSMO – mint, used either fresh or dried in salads, sauces, and stews.

DIPLES – a favorite teatime dessert. The dough is rolled very thin, cut in small pieces, and fried in hot oil. As one's hand becomes more practiced, the diples can be tied in bowknots or rolled in fancy shapes. Diples are served with syrup, cinnamon, and finely chopped nuts.

DOLMADAKIA – a dish made with grapevine leaves, which are stuffed and steamed. If the stuffing is rice, dolmadakia are served cold. If meat stuffing is used, they are served hot with avgolemono sauce.

DOMATES – tomatoes, which the Greeks love, especially spiced with cinnamon in stews or flavored with oregano in salads.

ENTRADA – a dish made with meat and vegetables.

FAKI – lentils; usually means lentil soup.

FASKOMILO – one of the Greek herb teas, said to be beneficial to colds and stomach ailments. They are very flavorful on their own merits.

FASSOULADA – a popular Greek dish. It is nourishing, tasty, and economical and provides, together with a salad, crusty bread, and a simple dessert, a complete meal.

FASSOULAKIA FRESKA – string beans. These may be left whole, cut, or sliced French-style. Frozen string beans, defrosted, may be substituted in these recipes.

FASSOULIA PIAZ – a salad made of cooked dried beans, onions, olive oil, and lemon juice; excellent for summer meals.

FAVA – a dish made of legumes, onion, and olive oil. Fava may be eaten warm or cold.

FAVA BEANS – fresh broad beans. In some markets, they are called fresh fava beans. Also available frozen.

FENIKIA – honey-dipped cookies, sometimes called *Melamakarona*. The recipe is said to have originated with the Venetians—hence the name.

FETA CHEESE – the favorite of the Greek cheeses. It is a white cheese made of goats' milk, with its own unusual flavor. Besides being served as an appetizer and table cheese, feta is used in making the various cheese and spinach-cheese bourekia.

FIDE – a fine pasta used primarily in soups.

FILO – *See* PHYLLO PASTRY.

FLAMOURI – another of the *tisanes*, or herb teas; *see* FASKOMILO.

FLOYERES – "flutes." This pastry, made of thin phyllo sheets, is rolled to resemble small flutes.

FRAPA – grapefruit.

GALATOBOUREKO – a pie made with phyllo pastry, a light cream custard, and syrup.

GALOPETA, GALOTOPETA – a cake made with milk; similar to a custard or custard pie.

GALOPOULO – turkey; always stuffed with one of the savory stuffings of Greek cookery.

GARIDES – shrimp.

GHOUDI – the brass mortar and pestle found in most Greek homes, used for pulverizing garlic and nuts for skordalia, pounding mahlepi to a fine powder, or mashing tarama with oil and lemon.

GHOUROUNAKI – a suckling pig.

GIOUVARLAKIA – small meatballs cooked in boiling stock. They are a thrifty, tasty family dinner. With the broth thickened, and flavored with avgolemono sauce, giouvarlakia move to the company-dinner category.

GIOUVETSI – a Greek specialty. Pieces of lamb are baked in the oven with tomato, onions, and garlic. Pasta is added to the casserole and, when it has cooked, the giouvetsi is served piping hot.

GLOSSA – a fish similar to flounder, used in Greece.

GLYKO, GLYKA – sweets or fruit preserves. A guest is offered a tray containing glyko in a small bowl, a glass of water, and a spoon. The custom is that he take a spoonful of glyko and the glass of water and wish his hostess good health.

GRAPEVINE LEAVES – used as the ingredient in dolmadakia. They are available in jars or cans in specialty stores.

HALVAH – a dessert made with farina and flavored with cinnamon. Halvah may be served warm or placed in a mold and chilled. Halvah made without butter is a good Lenten dessert.

HAMOMILO – another of the Greek herb teas; *see* FASKOMILO.

HAVIARI – caviar, black or red, served as an appetizer.

HIRINO – pork.

HORTA – salad greens and green vegetables, i.e. dandelion greens, chicory, lettuces, spinach, *etc.*

HUNKAR BEGENDI – a dish of lamb ragout and eggplant purée so delicious that "the king liked it."

IBRIK – *see* KAFEÏBRIKI.

IMAM BAILDI – a delicious dish made with eggplant, tomatoes, onions, garlic, parsley, and olive oil. There is an amusing story that gives this dish its name, "The priest (Imam) fainted." A famous Turkish Imam was very fond of eggplant. His wife was always thinking up new ways to serve the vegetable to him. One day she prepared this recipe, and the Imam found it so good that he fainted in ecstasy. (Two other reasons given are that the Imam fainted over the great amount of oil required in making this dish, and that he fainted because the dish was so rich.)

KADAIFE EKMEK – a dessert made of sweet bread or kadaife pastry baked in two layers and filled with a rich cream custard.

KADAIFE PASTRY – available in Greek bakery or confectionery shops. Kadaife is made of a batter that is poured into a perforated tin having about fifteen "teeth." This tin is held over a metal hot plate. As the batter is poured through the tin onto the hot metal, the kadaife partially cooks or dries into long thin strands resembling thin noodles or shredded wheat. The pastry is sold by the pound and is used to make the tasty kadaife desserts.

KAFEÏBRIKI – the special coffeepot used for making Greek or Turkish coffee. The pot is usually made of brass with a long handle, a narrow neck, and a wide mouth.

KAFES – Greek or Turkish coffee. The coffee beans are very finely ground or pulverized. The coffee must be brewed in a special coffee-pot, a kafeïbriki. This coffee is cooked with the sugar in it and, therefore, must be prepared or ordered to taste, i.e. medium sweet, very sweet, or bitter. Some coffee lovers insist on grinding their own coffee beans in a special mill, grinding just enough for the serving. This coffee is always served in demitasse.

KALAMARIA – squid. Kalamaria should be small to be tender. They are very good fried or stuffed with rice.

KAPAKOTI – a term for pot roasting. Literally translated, it means "with the cover on."

KAPAMA – a method of cooking meat or poultry, usually braised with onions, flavored with tomatoes and cinnamon, and simmered until done.

KARAMELA – caramel.

KARIDATA – nut cookies, somewhat similar to kourabiedes.

KARIDOPETA – a cake made with many eggs, ground nuts, and syrup. The cake is cut in diamond-shaped pieces.

KARPOUZI – watermelon, a favorite fruit in Greece.

KASSERI – a delicious table cheese. It is a creamy, firm cheese made of goats' milk, with a mild flavor. Fried or broiled kasseri with lemon juice is very good. Kasseri is also used in giouvetsi and stefado.

KEFALAKIA – a dish made with lambs' heads. Though the dish is not usual in this country, the meat is very tasty, and kefalakia is considered a specialty in Greek cookery.

KEFALOTIRI – a hard, salty cheese which grates easily. It is very good on all *pasta* dishes.

KEFTAIDES, KEFTAIDAKIA – Greek meatballs, which are made for all occasions. In small size, keftaidakia are used as appetizers for parties and festivities of every sort. Since they are equally good at room temperature, they are a "must" on picnics. In larger size, keftaides with pilaf, vegetable, and salad make a tasty family dinner.

KEKI – the term for cake, similar to layer cake.

KIMINO – cumin seed, an excellent addition to ground meat.

KOKKINA AVGA – red eggs, dyed for Easter.

KOKORETSI – the entrails and internal meats of the baby lamb, highly seasoned, baked or grilled over charcoal, and served with Easter dinner.

KOLOKITHAKIA, KOLOKITHIA – refers to summer squash, though zucchini is the type preferred in these recipes.

KOLOKITHOKEFTAIDES – squash fritters, made of mashed squash, eggs, parsley, and cheese and fried until golden brown.

KOLOKITHOPETA – a casserole made with layers of sliced squash, onions, and parsley.

KOLYVA – a traditional dish made by Greek families forty days after the death of a member of the family, again a year later, and then for the last time three years later. It is a combination of boiled wheat, white raisins, spices, and sugar.

KOTA – a fowl or roasting chicken.

KOTOPOULO – a small chicken, usually a fryer or a broiler.

KOUKIA – dried *fava* or lima beans.

KOUKIA FRESKA – fresh *fava* beans or fresh lima beans.

KOULOURAKIA – butter cookies, made in various shapes—little circles, small braids, tiny coils, figure eights, *etc*. The recipes make large amounts, but the cookies keep well (if you have a good hiding place).

KOUNOPEDI – cauliflower.

KOURABIEDES – the favorite cooky of the Greeks—a rich, short cooky covered with powdered sugar. They are made for all festive occasions.

KREAS – meat, though when the Greeks say "kreas" they usually mean lamb.

KREATOPETES – small meat pies. They are savory and a popular dish for Meat Fare Sunday.

KREMA – a custard or pudding. A bland krema is served on toast, flavored with cinnamon, for breakfast on May Day, May 1st.

KREMIDAKIA FRESKA – spring onions or scallions. Include as much of the green portion as is tender.

KREMIDAKIA, KREMIDIA – onions.

KRITHARAKI – fine barley or *orzo* used in many casseroles and soups.

KRITHAROSOUPA – barley soup.

KYTHONIA – quince. Quince is an all-purpose fruit for the Greeks. They are eaten when ripe, made into compotes and preserves, or featured at dinner with lamb or beef.

KYTHONOPASTO – quince preserves made into fancy shapes.

LADERES – foods braised in olive oil, simmered until done, and usually served cold or lukewarm.

LAHANO – cabbage.

LAHANODOLMADES – cabbage leaves stuffed with meat and rice and served warm. They make a tasty family dinner.

LAKERTHA – a pickled fish, usually made from the palamida. Canned lakertha is available in specialty shops. This fish, thinly sliced, makes an excellent meze.

LAMBRI – literally means "light" or "brightness." Refers to Easter.

LAMBROPSOMO – a sweet bread made at Easter time and decorated with red eggs.

LOUKANIKA – Greek sausages. These are served hot with lemon slices as a meze or fried with eggs and tomatoes.

LOUKOUMADES – sweet fritters fried in hot oil until golden brown and served warm with honey syrup and cinnamon; a quick and easy dessert.

LOUKOUMI – a Turkish sweet much favored in Greece and the Levant. It is a type of chewy candy with bits of pistachio or toasted almonds.

MACERITSA – the traditional soup eaten after the Resurrection Services on Easter morning to break the Lenten fast. This soup is made with the entrails and internal meats of the baby lamb and seasoned with spring onions, dill, and avgolemono sauce.

MAHLEPI – an unusual spice from Syria, which must be finely ground before using. It adds a delicious taste to cakes, cookies, *etc*. Mahlepi can be purchased in specialty shops.

MAÏTANO – parsley; frequently used in Greek cookery.

MAKARONADA – a dish of macaroni and meat sauce prepared in the Greek manner.

MANESTRA – a pasta similar to *orzo*.

MANTI – a meat pie.

MARIDES – smelts; tasty when fried.

MARINATA – the term for marinade or barbecue sauce.

MAROULIA – lettuce.

MASTICHA – a liqueur flavored with mastic. The term masticha also refers to the mastic itself, which is used as flavoring in cakes or cookies.

MAVRODAPHNE – a sweet dessert wine.

MELACHRINO XANTHO – literally translated means "brunette and blond" and is the name of a cake. The cake is made of a layer of yellow sponge and a layer of meringue mixed with finely chopped nuts; blond or brunette, it is delicious.

MELITZANES – eggplant; used in many varied dishes in Greek cookery.

MEZE, MEZETHAKIA – foods eaten as hors d'oeuvres to "stimulate the appetite." They accompany ouzo, masticha, or beer taken before a meal. However, this is a leisurely time for the Greeks, often an hour or two. Mezethakia are varied and well seasoned.

MIALA – lamb brains.

MIDIA – mussels. Though these shellfish require careful scraping and scrubbing before they are cooked, their flavor is well worth the effort.

MILO – apple. The fruits of Greece are excellent, and the favorite after-dinner dessert.

MIZITHRA – a mild cheese, excellent with *pasta* or as a table cheese. Hlori Mizithra, a soft, moist cheese, is available only in Greece.

MOUSSAKA – a meat-and-eggplant pie baked with a topping of rich cream sauce. It is a favorite dish of the Greeks and lends itself well to entertaining. Moussaka can be made ahead of time and rewarmed before serving. This dish is very rich; therefore the rest of the menu should be light.

NISIOTIKES – the Greek islands, or something native to the islands.

OKTAPODI – octopus, a popular dish in Greek cookery. Octopus has a flavor resembling lobster, and is even more tender. It has to be slowly pounded against a rock when first caught, as the flesh can be very tough and needs the pounding to make it tender. Since the fisherman does the pounding, any octopus purchased in a fish market should be ready to cook.

OREKTIKO, OREKTIKA – hors d'oeuvre. *See* MEZETHAKIA.

ORTHI – standing.

ORZO – a *pasta* used in many soups and main dishes; excellent for giouvetsi.

OUZO – a clear, aromatic spirit distilled from grapes and flavored with aniseed. When diluted with ice or water, ouzo becomes cloudy and white. As a newspaper columnist once said: "Ouzo becomes cloudy and you become gay."

PAÏDAKIA – lamb chops. Excellent broiled with chopped onions, oregano, salt, and pepper. Add lemon juice just before serving.

PALAMIDA – a large silver fish, very fat, with rich, heavy flesh. Its meat is not quite white and is often streaked with brown. Palamida comes from Africa to the Black Sea where it lays its eggs before returning again to Africa. It is caught in the Dardanelles. Palamida is served in many varied ways. Cod or haddock may be used in the same manner.

PANTESPANI – the Greek word for spongecake.

PANTZARIA – beets.

PAPAKI – a duckling.

PAPOUTSAKIA – literally translated, means "little shoes." This dish is made with eggplants of similar size. Filled with meat and lined up in a baking pan, the eggplants do resemble little shoes.

PASA MAKAROUNA – a baked dish of meat and homemade noodle dough, so named because it must be fit for a pasha or king.

PASKA, PASKALINO, PASKALINA – refers to Easter.

PASTA FLEURA – a very good rich pastry topped with cherry preserves and cut into small squares after baking.

PASTICHIO – a popular and often-served Greek dish. It is comprised of meat sauce, macaroni, cheese, and cream sauce. Pastichio is an excellent choice for the buffet table.

PATATES – potatoes.

PATSA – a soup made with pigs' feet, tripe, garlic, and egg and vinegar sauce. This tasty soup may be allowed to jell, served as an aspic, or may be served hot. In either case, hot red pepper is added to taste.

PAXIMADIA – sweet, biscuit-type cookies; excellent with coffee or tea.

PELTE – a thick syrup or pudding.

PHYLLO PASTRY – refers to the tissue paper-thin pastry used by the Greeks. Phyllo can be used for appetizers, luncheon or supper dishes, and fabulous desserts. Phyllo needs a practiced hand if made at home, but it is available in Greek bakery shops or specialty shops, and can be bought fresh or frozen.

PIAZ – bean salad.

PILAFI – a method of cooking rice. Long-grain rice is always used in pilafi. The liquid should be rich chicken stock. After the rice is done, a linen towel is placed over the saucepan and the lid is replaced. This helps absorb all excess moisture and leaves the rice "grain for grain."

PIPERIES – green peppers. These are stuffed by themselves or with other vegetables, with rice stuffing for a cold dish, or with meat and rice stuffing for a hot dish. They are also made into an appetizer and toursi, as well as used in salads.

PLAKI – a method of cooking, usually with onions, tomatoes, parsley, and olive oil. Though plaki is usually connected with fish, beans plaki and vegetable plaki are also made.

POLITA, POLITIKES – Constantinople, i.e. in the style of Constantinople cookery. During the Byzantine Empire, Constantinople, or New Rome, was noted for its culinary feats. An interesting story is told about the origin of the white chef's hat. The cooks of Constantinople were highly esteemed, and after the fall of the city most took refuge in the monasteries. There they continued their art, much to the delight of the monks. After a while the cooks felt that their habit should differ in some manner from the other monks', and received permission to don a white habit. The tall black hat of the monks became the tall white hat of the cooks, and over the years has become known as the symbol of the chef.

PORTOKALI – the Greek word for orange.

PRASA – leeks.

PSARI – fish. Since no part of Greece is far from the sea, fish is one of the favorite staples of Greek cookery.

PSAROSOUPA – fish soup. This dish may be eaten as a hearty soup, or, with the fish removed, provides two courses for the same meal.

PSITO – baked food.

PSOMI – bread.

RAVANI – favorite butter cake usually made with farina and flour and covered with a sugar syrup.

RETSINA – the national wine of Greece. Though the flavor is unusual, take the word of the Greeks and acquire a taste for it.

REVITHIA – chick-peas, which are cooked in the manner of dried legumes. Chick-peas are also roasted and salted and eaten as a meze.

RIGANATO, RIGANATA – term used for dishes seasoned with oregano.

RIZI – rice; usually long-grain rice is used in Greek cookery.

RIZOGALO – rice pudding.

ROMION or ROMI – rum.

SALATA – salad.

SALIANGKI – snails.

SALTSA – sauce; the Greeks are famous for their sauces.

SARAGLI – a type of nut-filled phyllo pastry rolled in long narrow rolls, shirred together, and poured over with syrup after baking. Saragli is similar in taste to baklava.

SARDELES and FILETO SARDELAS – sardines, served as appetizers whole or mashed with lemon juice.

SARMADES – the cabbage-and-pork rolls favored by the Macedonians or Kastorians. They are very rich and very tasty.

SAVORI – a dish that is highly spiced.

SELINO – celery. Use the chopped leaves as well as the stalks in these recipes.

SFOGATO – a type of soufflé of meat and squash. Sfogato may be served with tomato sauce for lunch or supper.

SIKOTAKI – lamb liver. Whether served yahni or fried with scallions, dill, and lemon juice, this is a very appetizing meat.

SKALTSOUNIA – turnovers filled with nuts or cheese and either fried or baked. Skaltsounia are popular in Crete.

SKORDALIA – a sauce made with garlic and thickened with potatoes, nuts, or bread. Lemon is indispensable to skordalia, and skordalia is indispensable to a variety of fried foods, i.e. fish, squash, and eggplants, as well as many other types of food.

SKOUMBRI, SKOUMBRIA – mackerel.

SMYRNAÏKO – a recipe originating in or favored by the people of Smyrna.

SOUPA AVGOLEMONO – the favorite of Greek soups. It is made with rich chicken broth (though lamb broth may be used also) and flavored with avgolemono sauce.

SOUR SALT – a salt similar to citric acid.

SOUSAME – sesame seed; used on bread, vasilopetes, and koulourakia.

SOUVLA – a skewer used for grilling.

SOUVLAKIA – small pieces of lamb threaded on a skewer with vegetables and grilled over charcoal.

SOUZOUKAKIA – meatballs flavored with cumin and garlic and shaped like little sausages.

SPANAKI – spinach.

SPANAKOPETA, SPANAKOPETES – the savory pastries made with phyllo, spinach, and cheese either as a pie or as small rolls or triangles.

SPANAKORIZO – a delicious combination of spinach and rice, equally good warm or cold.

STEFADO – a stew simmered slowly with onions, garlic, and vinegar. Stefado may be made with chicken, beef, lamb, or rabbit.

TARAMA – carp roe, sometimes called *botargo*. The egg is small and the color of the roe is a light orange. When mixed according to the recipe given for taramasalata, it becomes an excellent appetizer. Tarama is also used in taramokeftaides.

TARAMOKEFTAIDES – fritters made of tarama and potatoes. They are very tasty and make an excellent Lenten dish.

TARATORI – a cold soup, excellent for summer menus, made of yogurt or buttermilk. This soup is sometimes called *tzatziki*.

TAS KEBAB – small pieces of meat (*kebab*) cooked in a pot (*tas*). It is a type of ragout, or meat simmered in a thick sauce.

TIGHANITO, TIGHANITA – fried.

TIROPETA, TIROPETES, TIROPITAKIA – dishes or appetizers made with phyllo pastry, cheese, and eggs. These can be made into a pie or folded into small triangles or rolls. Either way is delicious, and all we can say is: be certain to make enough.

TIS SKARAS – broiled food.

TIS SMYRNIS – a recipe originating in or favored by the people of Smyrna.

TIS SOUVLAS – grilled food.

TOU FOURNOU – a dish baked in the oven.

TOURLOU – a term used for a stew of meat and many varied vegetables.

TOURSI – pickled vegetables and fruits—i.e. peppers, celery, cauliflower, olives, tomatoes, *etc.*—served as a relish. Toursi is also made with squid.

TOURTA – a butter cake.

TRAHANA – a homemade noodle dough used in soups and stews. Its flavor is unusual when made with yogurt or buttermilk. A commercial trahana is available in specialty stores.

TRIANTAFILLO GLYKO – rose petal preserves. Imported prepared rose petal preserves may be purchased at specialty shops if you do not wish to make your own.

TRIGONA – literally translated, means "triangles." These cookies, which are nut-filled phyllo pastry, are folded into small triangles.

TSIPOURA – resembles porgies. It is one of the favorite fish in Greece.

TSIRI – small, long, silver fish, which are dried. They are broiled, preferably on the coals out-of-doors as they have an unpleasant smell while cooking. But after marinating they are a very tasty appetizer.

TSOUREKI – an Easter cake sprinkled with sesame seeds and decorated with red eggs.

VARVARA – a dish similar to kolyva. Pomegranate seeds are added to varvara.

VASILOPETA – a cake made in honor of St. Basil, whose feast day is January 1st. Cakes differ in the various regions of Greece: some are a type of bread, others a type of rich yeast cake, others are flat, made of cooky dough, but all are good. And in each the custom of the coin for good luck to the finder and the ritual of cutting by the head of the house are the same.

VERIKOKO – apricot.

VISSINO – sour cherries, which are made into a tasty preserve.

VOTHINO – beef.

VOUTIRO – butter.

VRASTO – boiled or poached.

WOUDI – see GHOUDI.

XYSTO – grated.

YAHNI – a method of cooking. The food is braised with onions in olive oil, then water and sometimes tomatoes are added, and the food is simmered until done.

YEMISIS, YEMISTO – stuffing.

YEMISTA – a term used for vegetables stuffed with ground meat and rice and either simmered or baked until tender. These recipes make excellent family dinners.

YIALANDJI – a dish without meat, usually served cold.

YIAOURTI – yogurt, a type of soured milk made by adding the bacillus or culture to fresh milk. The Greeks claim many benefits from yogurt, including cure for stomach ailments and dyspepsia and a definite integral factor in longevity.

YIAOURTOPETA – a moist, light cake made with yogurt.

YOUVARLAKIA – see GIOUVARLAKIA.

ZESTI, ZESTO – hot.

ZOUMO – broth.

SOME SOURCES OF GREEK FOOD PRODUCTS

The house of Lekas & Drivas, Inc. is the first and oldest in the United States importing and distributing Greek Food Products. They also manufacture phyllo pastry packaged under the name of Filo. If your grocer does not carry Greek specialties, write for the name and address of the nearest store where you can buy them.

ADDRESS: Lekas & Drivas, Inc.
98 Fulton Street
Brooklyn 1, New York

Stores that stock Greek food and bakery products alphabetically according to state:

Bruno's Food Store
1218 South Sixth Avenue
Birmingham, Alabama

Cash Produce Co.
2223 Morris Avenue
Birmingham, Alabama

Niarhos Imp. Co.
1910 Morris Avenue
Birmingham, Alabama

Southway, c/o Simonetti Inc.
305 26th Avenue, West
North Birmingham, Alabama

Lignos Grocery
160 Government Street
Mobile, Alabama

C & K Imp. Co.
2771 West Pico Boulevard
Los Angeles, California

A & G Markets, Inc.
1807 Robinson Street
San Diego, California

Daldas Grocery
199 Eddy Street
San Francisco, California

Istanbul Pastry Co.
247 Third Street
San Francisco, California

Macy's
San Francisco, California

Seferi & Seferi
599 Lafayette Street
Bridgeport, Connecticut

Johnny's Market
5 New Britain Avenue
Hartford, Connecticut

Georgia's Sweet Shop
249 Arch Street
New Britain, Connecticut

Vittoria Imp. Co.
35 Lafayette Street
New Britain, Connecticut

New York Delicatessen
1207 Chapel Street
New Haven, Connecticut

Tom Apostolides
485 Pacific Street
Stamford, Connecticut

Impero Imp. Co.
181 Main Street
Waterbury, Connecticut

Aloupis Co.
916 9th Street, N.W.
Washington, D.C.

Olympia Imp. Co.
627 King Street
Wilmington, Delaware

Joseph's Imp. Food Co.
621 Fields Avenue
Jacksonville, Florida

Steve's Superette
1629 West Garden Street
Pensacola, Florida

Joseph Baratta
2503 S.W. 8th Street
Miami, Florida

Sidney's European Mkt.
710 Collins Avenue
Miami Beach, Florida

Maas Bros., Inc.—Dept. 810
1st Avenue North at 3rd Street
St. Petersburg, Florida

Angel's Market
455 Athens Street
Tarpon Springs, Florida

The Grecian Mart
3244 South Dixie Highway
   (U.S.1)
West Palm Beach, Florida

Big Apple Stores
1402 Highland Avenue
Atlanta, Georgia

George's Del.
1041 North Highland Avenue,
   N.E.
Atlanta, Georgia

Snack N Shop Del.
2118 North Decatur Plaza
Decatur, Georgia

Weiner's Super Mkt.
601 East 39th Street
Savannah, Georgia

Arimes Market
216 Walton Avenue
Lexington, Kentucky

John Louka Groc.
308 Dauphine Street
New Orleans, Louisiana

Throumoulos Market
75 Alfred Street
Biddeford, Maine

Boucouvalas Bros., Inc.
Common & Middle Streets
Saco, Maine

H & H Prod., Inc.
423 W. Lexington Avenue
Baltimore, Maryland

A. Rafaelides
501 Newkirk Street
Baltimore, Maryland

Blatsos Groc.
159 Summer Street
Lynn, Massachusetts

Euphrates Grocery
101 Shawmut Avenue
Boston, Massachusetts

Hellas Market
174 Broadway
Boston, Massachusetts

Laconia Groc.
908 Washington Street
Boston, Massachusetts

A & A Food Market
14 Central Square
Cambridge, Massachusetts

Demoulas Super Mkts.
80 Dummer Street
Lowell, Massachusetts

Giavis Market
391 Market Street
Lowell, Massachusets

Olympia Market
10 Spring Street
Worcester, Massachusetts

Big Ten Party Store
1928 Packard Road
Ann Arbor, Michigan

Warren Miller Mkt.
12700 West Warren
Dearborn, Michigan

Acropolis Market
8441 Joy Road
Detroit, Michigan

Delmar & Co.
501 Monroe Street
Detroit, Michigan

Mourad Groc. Co.
2410 Market Street
Detroit, Michigan

Leon's Food Mart, Inc.
2200 Winthrop Road
Lincoln, Nebraska

The Louis Cononelos Co.
McGill, Nevada

O. K. Fairbanks, Inc.
480 West Street
Keene, New Hampshire

Joseph's Bros.
118 Lake Avenue
Manchester, New Hampshire

New England Mkt.
144 Lake Avenue
Manchester, New Hampshire

Youngsville Mkt.
1536 Candia Road
Manchester, New Hampshire

Liamos Mkt.
176 West Pearl Street
Nashua, New Hampshire

Andrew's Del.
305 Sewell Avenue
Asbury Park, New Jersey

George's Food Market
25 South Kentucky Avenue
Atlantic City, New Jersey

Crest Del.
607 Central Avenue
East Orange, New Jersey

Kosmas Dourvekis
21 South Broad Street
Elizabeth, New Jersey

Central Food Stores
63 Main Street
Hackensack, New Jersey

Gacos Del.
378 Summit Avenue
Jersey City, New Jersey

James Magos
309 Grove Street
Jersey City, New Jersey

John's Del.
17 Washington Street
Morristown, New Jersey

Liberty Food Mkt.
52 West Market Street
Newark, New Jersey

Tom's Pork Store
791 South Orange Avenue
Newark, New Jersey

People's Grocery Co.
197 Neilson Street
New Brunswick, New Jersey

Italian Food Store
244 Smith Street
Perth Amboy, New Jersey

Village Shop Rite
9 South Orange Avenue
South Orange, New Jersey

S. Balish & Son
522 Morris Avenue
Summit, New Jersey

Napoli Food Mkt.
300 Hudson Street
Trenton, New Jersey

The Parthenon
3500 Central, S.E.
Albuquerque, New Mexico

L. Kontis
162 Hudson Avenue
Albany, New York

Ditmars & 35th St. Mkt.
28–07 Ditmars Boulevard
Astoria, New York

Empire Food Mkt.
29–05 23rd Avenue
Astoria, New York

†Kismet Oriental Pastry Shop
27–02 23rd Avenue
Astoria, New York

Constantine's Del.
205–10 48th Avenue
Bayside, New York

Panagos Bros.
187 Montrose Avenue
Brooklyn, New York

Sammy's Imp. & Dom. Foods
1348–1350 Hertel Avenue
Buffalo, New York

Hill's Super Mkts.
55 Motor Avenue
Farmingdale, New York

Freeport Ital. Amer. Del.
52 West Merrick Road
Freeport, New York

Dairy Fair Food Corp.
31 Station Plaza
Hempstead, New York

Kizmet Food Mkt.
13 Hilton Avenue
Hempstead, New York

Peter's Grocery
90–28 Parsons Boulevard
Jamaica, New York

Mineola Italian & Amer. Del.
160 Jericho Turnpike
Mineola, New York

†Anatoli Pastry Shop
401 West 40th Street
New York City

†Confectionery and bakery products only.

Athen's Food Market
542 Ninth Avenue
New York City

†Constantinople Pastry Shop
348 Eighth Avenue
New York City

Ethnikon Pastry Shop
532 Ninth Avenue
New York City

Kassos Bros.
570 Ninth Avenue
New York City

†Liberty-Oriental Pastry Shop
281 Audubon
New York City

Macy's
Herald Square
New York City

M. G. Couphopoulos
306 West 40th Street
New York City

Plaza Delicacy
54 West 58th Street
New York City

†Poseidon Confectionery Shop
629 Ninth Avenue
New York City

† Sugar N Spice Shop
8th Avenue Station at 42nd Street
New York City

H. C. Bohack Co., Inc. Stores

Dilbert's Super Markets

C. A. Thanos & Co.
424 Pearl Street
Syracuse, New York

George Kakaris
402 East Trade Street
Charlotte, North Carolina

Camel City Groc.
303 Church Street
Winston-Salem, North Carolina

Table Supply Food Store
Cameron Village
Raleigh, North Carolina

Nick Yanko's
846 West Market Street
Akron, Ohio

O'Neil's Epicure Shop
226 South Main—Dept. 854
Akron, Ohio

Canton Imp. Co.
123 Cherry Avenue, S.E.
Canton, Ohio

Tom's Delicatessen
433 South High Street
Columbus, Ohio

Crystal A. G. Food Ctr.
601 Main Street
Martins Ferry, Ohio

Maletis Bros.
100 N.W. 3rd Avenue
Portland, Oregon

Bournias & Englesson
416 East 3rd Street
Bethlehem, Pennsylvania

Capitol Italian Groc.
213 Chestnut Street
Harrisburg, Pennsylvania

Michael's Mkt.
230 South 10th Street
Philadelphia, Pennsylvania

European Groc. Store
520 Court Place
Pittsburgh, Pennsylvania

Daniel's Coffee & Tea
320 Penn Street
Reading, Pennsylvania

Adelphia Imp. Co.
44 North Main Street
Wilkes Barre, Pennsylvania

Tom English
72 Pawtucket Avenue
Pawtucket, Rhode Island

John Liatos
458 Meeting Street
Charleston, South Carolina

The Cheese Market
505 Clinch Avenue, S.W.
Knoxville, Tennessee

Louis Paletta Grocery
425 North Santa Rosa at Martin
San Antonio, Texas

Kandis Liq. & Imports
1202 North Main Street
Victoria, Texas

Seven Day Shopping Center
Barracks Road at Route 29, North
Charlottesville, Virginia

Galanides, Inc.
902 Cooke Avenue
Norfolk, Virginia

Greek American Imp. Co.
518–520 East Marshall Street
Richmond, Virginia

The New Yorker Del.
2602 Williamson Road
Roanoke, Virginia

Nick Carras
422 North 48th Street
Seattle, Washington

A. G. Food Center
2201 Market Street
Wheeling, West Virginia

GREEK ORTHODOX CALENDAR
OF MAJOR FEASTS AND HOLIDAYS

JANUARY
1   Day of St. Basil the Great
6   †Day of Epiphany or Theophany, the Baptism of Christ
7   Day of St. John the Baptist
17   Day of St. Anthony the Great
18   Day of St. Athanasios and St. Cyril
20   Day of St. Euthemios
25   Day of St. Gregory the Theologian
30   Day of the Three Hierarchs: St. Basil the Great
                                 St. Gregory the Theologian
                                 St. John the Chrysostom

FEBRUARY
2   †Hypapante Candlemas—Presentation of Christ at the Temple
10   Day of St. Haralambos
17   Day of St. Theodore

PRE-LENT
1st Sunday: Sunday of Publican and Pharisee
2nd Sunday: Sunday of the Prodigal Son
3rd Sunday: Meat Fare Sunday (Apokreos)
4th Sunday: Cheese Fare Sunday

THE GREAT LENT: Seven weeks before Easter
Pure Monday: First day of Lent
1st Friday of Lent: 1st stanza of Laudations to Virgin Mary
1st Sunday of Lent: Sunday of Orthodoxy
2nd Friday of Lent: 2nd stanza of Laudations to Virgin Mary
3rd Friday of Lent: 3rd stanza of Laudations to Virgin Mary
3rd Sunday of Lent: Adoration of the Holy Cross
4th Friday of Lent: 4th stanza of Laudations to Virgin Mary
5th Friday of Lent: Akathist Hymn—Complete four stanzas of Lauda-
                    tions to Virgin Mary
†Palm Sunday

MARCH
9   Day of Forty Martyrs
25 †Annunciation of the Virgin Mary
     Greek Independence Day

APRIL
23 Day of St. George
25 Day of St. Mark

HOLY WEEK
Palm Sunday (evening): Nymphios Service
Holy Monday (evening): Nymphios Service
Holy Tuesday (evening): Nymphios Service
Holy Wednesday: Sacrament of Holy Unction
Holy Thursday: Dedicated to the Last Supper (Morning)
                       Dedicated to the Crucifixion (Evening)
                       Reading of the Twelve Gospels
Good Friday: Dedicated to the death and burial of Christ
Holy Saturday: Dedicated to the descent of Christ into Hades

§EASTER SUNDAY: Dedicated to the Resurrection of Christ
1st Friday After Easter: Day of Zoodochos Peghe—Life Giving Fountain
1st Sunday after Easter: Sunday of St. Thomas
2nd Sunday after Easter: Sunday of the Myrrh-Bearing Women
3rd Sunday after Easter: Sunday of the Paralytic
4th Sunday after Easter: Sunday of the Samaritan Woman
5th Sunday after Easter: Sunday of the Blind Man
Forty days after Easter: †The Lord's Ascension
6th Sunday after Easter: Sunday of the Holy Fathers
7th Sunday after Easter: †Holy Pentecost Sunday

MAY
2 Day of St. Athanasius
8 Day of St. John the Theologian
21 Day of St. Constantine and St. Helen

JUNE
29 Day of the Holy Apostles, St. Peter and St. Paul
30 Feast of the Twelve Apostles

JULY
20 Day of the Prophet Elias
25 Repose of St. Anna

26 Day of St. Paraskevi
27 Day of St. Panteleimon

AUGUST
1 Beginning of the Fast of the Virgin Mary
6 †Transfiguration of Christ
15 †The Assumption of the Virgin Mary

SEPTEMBER
8 †Nativity of the Theotokos
14 †Elevation of the Holy Cross (Fast Day)
16 Day of St. Euphemia

OCTOBER
18 Day of St. Luke the Evangelist
20 Day of St. Gerasimos
23 Day of St. Iakovos the Apostle
26 Day of St. Demetrios

NOVEMBER
1 Day of St. Cosmas and St. Damianos
8 Day of the Archangels Michael and Gabriel
13 Day of St. John the Chrysostom
14 Day of St. Phillip
15 Beginning of the Fast of the Nativity
16 Day of St. Matthew the Apostle
21 †Presentation of the Holy Theotokos
25 Day of St. Catherine
30 Day of St. Andrew

DECEMBER
4 Day of St. Barbara
6 Day of St. Nicholas
12 Day of St. Spyridon
15 Day of St. Eleutherios
25 †Christmas Day
27 Day of St. Stephen

† One of the twelve most important Orthodox Feast Days
§ Greatest Festival of the Greek Orthodox Church year
Every Wednesday and Friday of the year—with the exception of Wednesday and Friday after Christmas and after Easter—are fast days.
Christmas Eve marks the beginning of twelve days of celebration in the Greek Orthodox Church.

. . . AND ON TO GREECE TODAY!

The landscapes of Greece and the Greek islands defy description in their variety and contrast. There are snow-capped mountains and far-flung olive and citrus groves, rocky valleys and precipices, azure seascapes and lush semitropical vegetation. The whitewashed villages of a seafaring people contrast with the rugged gray and brown stone coastlines that are crowned with Frankish and Venetian fortresses and with ancient temples glowing from white to bronze above an ancient sea which ranges from turquoise to sapphire by way of aquamarine.

But it is really the people who give the kingdom its magic aura. Proud of their country's past, anxious to help build its future, hard-working, dignified, friendly, and extroverted, the modern Greeks are true sophisticates.

The visitor will enjoy the cordial atmosphere and hospitable spirit that have characterized the Greek race for thousands of years. The word *"xenos"* means both stranger and guest; it clearly denotes the people's natural tendency to consider every stranger an impatiently awaited friend. Writers of other nationalities have often praised Greek hospitality, an age-old tradition that surmounts language barriers to make the friendly stranger welcome. Traditionally seafaring, the Greeks are international-minded and cosmopolitan in their outlook. They are courteous, generous, and perfect hosts. All the world may come to see them without changing their indelible character.

In Greece the survival of historic spots that witnessed the birth of many charming myths gives the country an appeal not to be found elsewhere. Yet myth and history are intertwined. In 1870, solely on the strength of Homer's texts, Heinrich Schliemann, the German archaeologist, made legend into history with the discovery of Troy.

The mainland of Greece is, for the most part, mountainous and endowed with a jagged coastline. The easternmost tip of Attica, surrounded by the sea, is the setting for Athens and its magnificent

Acropolis. The Parthenon—"the ideal crystallized in Pentelic marble"—visible from any part of the city, seems to soar as the primary symbol of Greek culture. This masterpiece, even in its ruined state, imposes calm and serenity on the spectator. Ancient monuments however, are not the sole aspect of Athens today—a gay, cosmopolitan city, combining lightheartedness with a sense of tradition. Its sights encompass the tiny, candlelit Byzantine churches, the lovely palace gardens, the squares filled with people sitting outside the cafés, sipping tiny cups of thick black coffee and tall glasses of water, talking and gesticulating in perpetual, inconclusive argument. For this is Greece, a hub of individual thought —a sharp-witted, subtle, people—mischievous spectators whose critical minds relish satires on their own and foreign customs or jokes at the expense of powers that be.

But apart from Athens, Greece is a country that repays exploration. Excellent roads, multilingual Greek guides thoroughly versed in Greek mythology, history, literature, and plastic arts, and guided tours aboard buses or small vessels facilitate the visitor's travels.

Delphi, the sacred precinct of the ancient Greeks, where Apollo spoke through his oracle, still casts its spell of mystery. Nature joins in enhancing the brooding drama with craggy mountains and a deep valley, lending credence to the belief of the ancients that a stone at Delphi was the earth's navel. Snow-capped Olympus, in Thessaly, where laughter-loving gods feasted on nectar and ambrosia, is surely the most wondrous name in Greek mythology. Seeing the Meteora (meaning "hovering between heaven and earth")—the Greek Orthodox monasteries built in the fourteenth century atop needlelike crags—the viewer can almost believe that the gods still live on Olympus. Two of the monasteries are closed to women, but at St. Stephen's the monks welcome all visitors in accordance with the traditions of Greek hospitality.

In the Peloponnessus, the southern peninsula of Greece separated from the mainland by the Corinth Canal, the visitor encounters a mysterious, dramatic atmosphere filled with the aura of legend and myth. The ancient towns of Corinth and Mycenae bring to mind the dramas of Sophocles and Euripides, Olympia, where Greeks competed in the Sacred Games, and Epidaurus, whose theater, built in the fourth century B.C., seats 14,000, and whose acoustics have never been surpassed. The public throngs to see the ancient tragedies on the selfsame sites where they were enacted in the past—Epidaurus, Delphi, Athens. No other theaters in the world offer settings as resplendent. The audiences are swept by enthusiasm as they are transported back to the days of gods and heroes.

The Greek islands are sprinkled around the mainland like steppingstones in the sapphire sea. In the Ionian Islands, located in the Ionian Sea, is Corfu, an island of luxurious flowers and sensual greenness, the setting of which might well have inspired Homer. The Cyclades, in the Aegean Sea, include Mykonos, with its cube-shaped houses and domed churches—as many as there are days in the year—and Delos, the sacred island of Apollo, with the white Naxos lions guarding the birthplace of the god. The Dodecanese, restored to Greece after World War II, include the beautiful island of Rhodes, with its sweep of beaches and its blend of Doric and Ionian temples, Frankish, Crusader, and Venetian fortresses, and Turkish mosques and minarets; Kos, where Hippocrates composed the oath which has bound physicians ever since and where his tree still grows in the square; and Patmos, the island to which St. John the Divine was exiled and where he had his vision of the Apocalypse. The monastery of St. John the Divine contains a magnificent and extremely renowned Gospel according to St. Mark, illuminated throughout in gold and silver on purple parchment (a reminder that the Bible was first written in Greek). The island of Crete is the principal Mediterranean crossroads for Greece, Asia Minor, and Egypt. The heart of Crete is Knossos, whose Palace of Minos with its magnificent frescoes reveals a civilization existing between the fourteenth and fifteenth centuries B.C. that achieved a harmonious balance between utilitarian activities, artistic pleasures, sports (the Cretans invented bullfighting), and the acme of comfort.

Through thirty centuries of history, the Greeks have perpetuated the image of what is perhaps the wisest and most agreeable civilization of all time. Greece is ageless, the ancient and modern are united within her in perfect harmony, and she will welcome the friendly visitor with open arms.

BEN F. CARRUTHERS
Vice President, Bennett Associates
New York City

INDEX

M